Japanese
Kanji
AND
Kana
WORKBOOK

WOLFGANG HADAMITZKY & MARK SPAHN

TUTTLE Publishing

Tokyo | Rutland, Vermont | Singapore

"Books to Span the East and West"

Tuttle Publishing was founded in 1832 in the small New England town of Rutland, Vermont [USA]. Our core values remain as strong today as they were then—to publish best-in-class books which bring people together one page at a time. In 1948, we established a publishing outpost in Japan—and Tuttle is now a leader in publishing English-language books about the arts, languages and cultures of Asia. The world has become a much smaller place today and Asia's economic and cultural influence has grown. Yet the need for meaningful dialogue and information about this diverse region has never been greater. Over the past seven decades, Tuttle has published thousands of books on subjects ranging from martial arts and paper crafts to language learning and literature—and our talented authors, illustrators, designers and photographers have won many prestigious awards. We welcome you to explore the wealth of information available on Asia at www.tuttlepublishing.com.

Published by Tuttle Publishing, an imprint of Periplus Editions (HK) Ltd.

www.tuttlepublishing.com

Copyright © 2017 by Periplus Editions (HK) Ltd
Database publishing & typesetting: Seiko Harada and Rainer Weihs, Berlin
All rights reserved.

LCC Card No. 91-65055
ISBN 978-4-8053-1448-7

First edition, 1991
Revised edition, 2017

Distributed by:

North America, Latin America & Europe
Tuttle Publishing
364 Innovation Drive
North Clarendon,
VT 05759-9436 U.S.A.
Tel: 1 (802) 773-8930
Fax: 1 (802) 773-6993
info@tuttlepublishing.com
www.tuttlepublishing.com

Japan
Tuttle Publishing
Yaekari Building, 3rd Floor
5-4-12 Osaki Shinagawa-ku
Tokyo 141 0032
Tel: (81) 3 5437-0171
Fax: (81) 3 5437-0755
sales@tuttle.co.jp
www.tuttle.co.jp

Asia Pacific
Berkeley Books Pte. Ltd.
3 Kallang Sector #04-01
Singapore 349278
Tel: (65) 6741-2178
Fax: (65) 6741-2179
inquiries@periplus.com.sg
www.tuttlepublishing.com

27 26 25 24 23   13 12 11 10 9 8 7   2305MP
Printed in Singapore

TUTTLE PUBLISHING® is a registered trademark of Tuttle Publishing, a division of Periplus Editions (HK) Ltd.

CONTENTS

Introduction

The purpose of this *Japanese Kanji & Kana Workbook* is to help students of Japanese master writing the two phonetic kana syllabaries (46 hiragana and 46 katakana) and 617 basic kanji characters from the official Jōyō Kanji list.

With so many characters, it is important to study them systematically, in a carefully thought-out progression. This workbook answers the need for a step-by-step presentation of characters by largely following the system developed in the book *Japanese Kanji and Kana*[1]. This order of presentation is based on pedagogical principles, proceeding from simple, frequent kanji to those that are more complex and occur less often.

For learners who are preparing for the international Japanese-Language Proficiency Test (JLPT) or for the Advanced Placement (AP) Japanese Language and Culture Exam, the 617 kanji are divided into the first three levels of the JLPT, from N5 (80 kanji) through N4 (167 kanji) to N3 (370 kanji). This will also help to break down the large number of kanji into subsets that are easier to work with. The kanji that this book lists in the three levels follow documents previously provided by the Japan Foundation, which however no longer specifies just which kanji will be tested in each level. But it can be anticipated that there will be no great changes in the selection and number of kanji the test taker will be quizzed on. This book is intended both for self-study and as a classroom resource.

Each kanji is accompanied by information about it: its stroke sequence, up to three graphic elements that contribute to its meaning and pronunciation, its officially recognized readings, its most important definitions, and up to four useful compounds in which the kanji appears. For maximum benefit to learners who study the kanji in sequence, the compounds use only kanji that have been introduced earlier.

Characters are presented in brush, pen, and printed form. Each character in pen form is printed in light gray for you to trace over. These gray strokes will guide your hand the first time you try writing a new character and will help you quickly develop a feel for the proper proportions.

When practicing writing the characters, don't forget that they should be written to fit into squares, either real or imaginary, of exactly the same size. The *Japanese Kanji & Kana Workbook* has convenient, preprinted squares, of both large and normal size for all kana and for kanji 1 through 247 (levels N5 and N4), and of normal size only for kanji 248 through 617 (level N3).

The best way to begin learning the Japanese writing system is to start with one of the two syllabaries, either hiragana or katakana. This is because:

1. The number of characters is limited to 46 characters per syllabary.
2. The forms of the characters are simple (one to four strokes per kana).
3. Each character has only one pronunciation (except for two characters that each have two readings).
4. The kana syllabaries represent the entire phonology of the Japanese language, which means that any text can be written entirely in kana, without using any kanji at all.

It is difficult to say which syllabary should be learned first. If you learn katakana first, even as a beginner you will be able to write many words, especially loan-words from English, that you already know. Hiragana, however, is by far the more frequently used syllabary. We recommend the following learning sequence as the quickest way to master hiragana or katakana.

1. Divide either syllabary into **several small units**. Concentrate on only a few kana in each session. Begin, for instance, with the first five vowels of hiragana.

[1] Wolfgang Hadamitzky and Mark Spahn: *Japanese Kanji and Kana. A Complete Guide to the Japanese Writing System.* TUTTLE Publishing, Tokyo | Rutland, Vermont | Singapore, Third edition, 2012.

2. Practice the **pronunciation** of each kana, first while looking at the transcription and later without looking. This will help you link the sound of each kana to its visual image.
3. Memorize the **order of the syllables** (*a-i-u-e-o, ka-ki-ku-ke-ko*) by reading them aloud. (Later, to learn the alphabetical sequence of the whole syllabary, memorize the syllables at the beginning of each row: *a-ka-sa-ta-na, ha-ma-ya-ra-wa*.)
4. Memorize the **shape** of each kana and compare it to that of other kana; take notice of similarities and differences.
5. Memorize the **order** in which the strokes are written and the **direction** in which each stroke is written.
6. **Practice writing** each kana, first writing on the two gray pen forms in the large squares. Practice each kana until you can write it with the correct stroke order, stoke direction, and proportions without looking at the model.
7. Read aloud and **write all the words** that are given as examples for each character.
8. After finishing all the characters of either the hiragana or katakana syllabary, **review** them to check your grasp of forms and sounds.
9. **Repeat** the above steps for each unit.
10. **Review, and train yourself to read quickly**. To enhance your ability to quickly recognize all the kana and kanji in this workbook we recommend using the game and tutorial program *Kanji in Motion*[2]. The object is to make as fast as possible a connection between characters swirling on a screen and the corresponding readings and meanings shown on the side.

When memorizing kanji, use the same method as the one recommended above for the syllabaries. For kanji, look at the **basic graphic elements** (radical and graphemes) the entry is made up of; you will soon notice that all kanji are constructed from relatively few basic elements. These elements often indicate the meaning and/or pronunciation of the kanji. Instead of following the order of kanji presented in this workbook, you can choose any order you like. You might, for example, select the order in which kanji are introduced in the textbook you're using in class. The disadvantage to this, however, is that the compounds listed under a given kanji will then contain characters that you have not yet learned.

The rules as described in the preceding paragraphs are for writing characters by hand with a conventional writing implement like a pencil or pen. In practice, however, there are as many variations in writing as there are in other written languages – variations in handwritten forms and printed fonts that can make it difficult for learners to recognize and read kanji.

In this workbook we cover only the standard, non-calligraphic script taught in schools and seen in books and newspapers. But to point out the slight differences within this standard, all the kanji listed in the main part of this book appear in three styles: the head-kanji as a model for copying (with the strokes labeled with little numbers to indicate in what direction and order they are to be written), a handwritten form, and, in the compounds, a standard printed form. The length and orientation (horizontal, vertical, slanting) of the strokes should be noted as well as the direction and sequence in which they are written.

When counting strokes, be aware that printed kanji sometimes appear to be written with a different number of strokes than the number they are actually written with by hand. In particular, the following components have the following stroke-counts:

了	子	阝	辶	比	𧘇	臣
(1)	(2)	(2)	(2)	(4)	(4)	(7)

The kanji in this workbook are fully indexed by *on-kun* readings and by radical. Page 288 gives a list of the 79 radicals used in the Index by Radicals, while inside the back cover you will find a Checklist for Determining the Radical of a Character.

[2] Wolfgang Hadamitzky and Mark Spahn: *Kanji in Motion*. 2017.

Kana and Kanji Overview Lists

Hiragana (p. 11–33)

printed form	pen form
あいうえお かきくけこ さしすせそ たちつてと なにぬねの はひふへほ まみむめも やゆよ らりるれろ わん	あいうえお かきくけこ さしすせそ たちつてと なにぬねの はひふへほ まみむめも やゆよ らりるれろ わん

Katakana (p. 34–56)

printed form	pen form
アイウエオ カキクケコ サシスセソ タチツテト ナニヌネノ ハヒフヘホ マミムメモ ヤユヨ ラリルレロ ワヲン	アイウエオ カキクケコ サシスセソ タチツテト ナニヌネノ ハヒフヘホ マミムメモ ヤユヨ ラリルレロ ワヲン

80 kanji N5 (p. 57–96)

人	一	二	三	日	四	五	六	七	八	九	十	円	百	千	万	月	火	水	木
1	2	3	4	5	6	7	8	9	10	11	12	13	14	15	16	17	18	19	20
金	土	本	大	小	中	雨	下	上	川	山	分	国	時	間	生	年	前	後	午
21	22	23	24	25	26	27	28	29	30	31	32	33	34	35	36	37	38	39	40
先	今	入	出	休	見	聞	語	行	来	東	西	北	南	左	右	名	外	半	長
41	42	43	44	45	46	47	48	49	50	51	52	53	54	55	56	57	58	59	60
男	女	子	電	学	母	父	校	毎	書	車	気	天	高	白	話	読	友	食	何
61	62	63	64	65	66	67	68	69	70	71	72	73	74	75	76	77	78	79	80

167 kanji N4 (p. 97–180)

明	曜	風	田	切	以	口	目	手	足	体	自	言	方	物	事	夕	死	週	不
81	82	83	84	85	86	87	88	89	90	91	92	93	94	95	96	97	98	99	100
発	心	思	力	安	用	字	文	海	地	立	私	公	意	元	工	空	理	少	道
101	102	103	104	105	106	107	108	109	110	111	112	113	114	115	116	117	118	119	120
通	場	主	住	会	答	問	員	者	家	室	屋	店	古	新	親	質	紙	町	京
121	122	123	124	125	126	127	128	129	130	131	132	133	134	135	136	137	138	139	140
同	色	黒	赤	青	的	知	強	医	族	旅	肉	重	多	品	動	野	売	買	教
141	142	143	144	145	146	147	148	149	150	151	152	153	154	155	156	157	158	159	160
早	茶	世	花	代	有	別	正	業	犬	牛	特	駅	鳥	洋	魚	急	悪	味	社
161	162	163	164	165	166	167	168	169	170	171	172	173	174	175	176	177	178	179	180
銀	帰	料	飲	飯	館	使	仕	図	計	画	音	映	英	題	注	楽	作	起	度
181	182	183	184	185	186	187	188	189	190	191	192	193	194	195	196	197	198	199	200
病	歌	開	弟	兄	姉	妹	去	真	走	歩	転	集	運	送	近	持	待	界	終
201	202	203	204	205	206	207	208	209	210	211	212	213	214	215	216	217	218	219	220

冬 春 夏 秋 朝 昼 夜 止 台 始 堂 試 験 写 考 漢 習 院 着 服
221 222 223 224 225 226 227 228 229 230 231 232 233 234 235 236 237 238 239 240

広 勉 貸 借 建 究 研
241 242 243 244 245 246 247

370 kanji N3 (p. 181 – 273)

耳 身 取 当 石 内 部 全 回 性 好 交 他 位 法 和 原 光 相 想
248 249 250 251 252 253 254 255 256 257 258 259 260 261 262 263 264 265 266 267

首 路 所 信 合 点 局 居 民 宅 宿 市 番 術 都 付 共 供 向 両
268 269 270 271 272 273 274 275 276 277 278 279 280 281 282 283 284 285 286 287

満 平 実 情 約 引 米 数 類 種 働 労 務 活 続 育 流 草 葉 化
288 289 290 291 292 293 294 295 296 297 298 299 300 301 302 303 304 305 306 307

変 愛 受 成 感 最 号 在 存 表 面 頭 顔 産 馬 議 論 王 現 単
308 309 310 311 312 313 314 315 316 317 318 319 320 321 322 323 324 325 326 327

戦 争 末 未 申 神 失 夫 婦 支 科 良 反 官 利 便 任 権 調 演
328 329 330 331 332 333 334 335 336 337 338 339 340 341 342 343 344 345 346 347

絵 給 暗 定 決 薬 昨 段 由 対 曲 記 得 役 船 渡 席 欠 次 職
348 349 350 351 352 353 354 355 356 357 358 359 360 361 362 363 364 365 366 367

能 可 予 形 閉 関 説 美 様 師 商 過 適 程 組 要 具 直 値 置
368 369 370 371 372 373 374 375 376 377 378 379 380 381 382 383 384 385 386 387

制 徒 伝 進 連 返 阪 遠 園 達 期 招 寒 解 歯 歳 政 果 守 治
388 389 390 391 392 393 394 395 396 397 398 399 400 401 402 403 404 405 406 407

常 非 束 速 勝 負 敗 放 配 酒 害 割 必 乗 式 機 飛 険 危 探
408 409 410 411 412 413 414 415 416 417 418 419 420 421 422 423 424 425 426 427

深 与 老 若 苦 経 済 才 財 因 難 困 勤 婚 等 雑 殺 命 念 願
428 429 430 431 432 433 434 435 436 437 438 439 440 441 442 443 444 445 446 447

払 皆 談 確 観 覚 規 側 列 例 完 示 際 察 礼 祖 助 状 太 陽
448 449 450 451 452 453 454 455 456 457 458 459 460 461 462 463 464 465 466 467

客 格 熱 残 然 容 責 積 差 精 晴 静 破 港 妻 亡 望 初 識 幸
468 469 470 471 472 473 474 475 476 477 478 479 480 481 482 483 484 485 486 487

報 辞 告 洗 窓 遅 警 御 加 参 増 富 求 球 件 晩 許 認 絶 賛
488 489 490 491 492 493 494 495 496 497 498 499 500 501 502 503 504 505 506 507

声 費 資 貧 収 易 留 昔 散 備 込 横 座 君 選 舞 夢 違 冷 落
508 509 510 511 512 513 514 515 516 517 518 519 520 521 522 523 524 525 526 527

消 退 限 眠 景 緒 幾 犯 罪 捕 突 到 倒 誤 互 係 慣 煙 鳴 浮
528 529 530 531 532 533 534 535 536 537 538 539 540 541 542 543 544 545 546 547

候 降 雪 登 迷 彼 押 越 遊 更 構 打 投 断 判 優 悲 指 偉 迎
548 549 550 551 552 553 554 555 556 557 558 559 560 561 562 563 564 565 566 567

余 除 途 靴 寝 箱 盗 庭 欲 処 喜 髪 杯 追 訪 泳 刻 笑 戻 息
568 569 570 571 572 573 574 575 576 577 578 579 580 581 582 583 584 585 586 587

否 呼 吹 吸 背 腹 包 痛 疲 寄 忙 忘 福 折 暮 頂 掛 猫 似 頼
588 589 590 591 592 593 594 595 596 597 598 599 600 601 602 603 604 605 606 607

疑 逃 努 怒 恐 偶 恥 抜 娘 怖
608 609 610 611 612 613 614 615 616 617

Rules for Writing Kanji

Before beginning to write a kanji, take a look at its structure and components and its meanings and readings. You will then better understand what you are writing and why it is to be written as described. As you write the kanji, try also to write a word – more precisely, a reading and meaning – to associate with it, as you would when vocabulary-building in your own language. This will help you fix the character in your memory and recognize it upon seeing it again.

When you feel you can reproduce the kanji from memory, write the compounds in which it occurs with the readings you have learned. Compounds are important as mini-context for going beyond the acquisition of individual characters. They will increase your vocabulary while getting you to review previously learned kanji.

The small sequential numbers at the beginning of each stroke in the following examples and in the main part of the book indicate, as with the kana, the direction in which each stroke is to be written and the order in which the strokes of a kanji are to be written; the last number gives the total number of strokes in the kanji.

The table inside the front cover summarizes the most important rules for writing kanji.

1. Stroke direction

Horizontal stroes are written from left to right:

Vertical and slanting strokes are written from top to bottom:

An exception is the combination of a short slanting down-stroke followed by a short slanting up-stroke, as in the radicals *sanzui* 氵, *nisui* 冫, and *yamaidare* 疒 and in 求 and similar kanji:

A stroke may change direction several times:

2. Stroke order

a. From top to bottom:

二 工

b. From left to right:

川 竹

c. Middle stroke before short flanking side-strokes:

小 当 水

But:

d. With intersecting strokes, horizontal before vertical:

十 土 七

Exceptions:

田 王 催

e. With X-forming strokes, from upper right to lower left, then from upper left to lower right:

8

f. A piercing vertical stroke is written last:

中 申 車 半 聿 平
手

If the vertical middle stroke does not protrude above or below, the sequence of strokes is: upper part, then middle stroke, then lower part:

里 里

g. A piercing horizontal stroke is written last:

女 子 母 舟

h. First the vertical stroke, then the short horizontal stroke that adjoins it on the right:

上 正 足 走

i. First the left and upper part of an outer enclosure:

国 回 匝 同 司 内
風

But:

区 医

j. A lower-left enclosure is written last:

進 直

Explanation of the Character Entries

Hiragana/Katakana

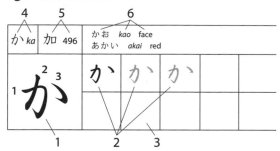

1. The kana character in brush form, with numbers showing stroke order positioned at the beginning of each stroke.

2. Three squares with the kana character in pen form, the latter two printed in light gray as a practice template to trace over.
3. Empty squares in which to write first the kana character and then the example words.
4. The kana character in printed form, with pronunciation in roman letters.
5. Kanji from which the kana character is derived, with the reference number of that kanji.
6. Up to four common words, with romanization and meanings. These words contain only kana that have already been introduced.

Kanji

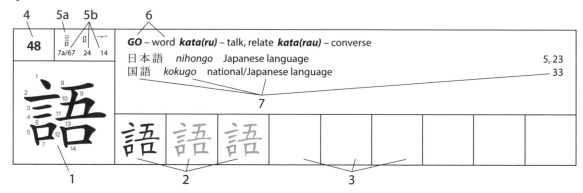

1. The kanji character in brush form, with numbers showing stroke order positioned at the beginning of each stroke.
2. Three squares with the kanji in pen form, the latter two printed in light gray as a practice template to trace over.
3. Empty squares in which to write the entry kanji and compounds.
4. Number of the kanji in this workbook.
5a. Radical with its number-and-letter "descriptor", under which the kanji is listed in the Index by Radicals and in *The Kanji Dictionary*[3].
5b. Up to three graphemes (basic elements) with their reference number, under which the kanji can be retrieved in the forthcoming character

dictionary *KanjiVision*[4]. A slash appears before the grapheme number (/67) if the first grapheme is the same as the radical in the printed character dictionaries that use the 79-radical system.
6. *On* readings, in capital italics; *kun* readings, in lowercase italics; readings that are infrequent or used only in special cases, in brackets; *okurigana* (part of a word that is written in kana), in parentheses; English meanings. All officially recognized readings of the kanji are listed.
7. Compounds, with romanization, meanings, and cross-reference numbers to the main entries for other kanji in the compound.

---

[3] Mark Spahn and Wolfgang Hadamitzky: *The Kanji Dictionary. Find Any Compound Using Any of Its Component Characters.* TUTTLE Publishing, Tokyo | Rutland, Vermont | Singapore, 1996.

[4] Wolfgang Hadamitzky and Mark Spahn: *KanjiVision. Online Character Dictionary*, 2017.

| あ *a* | 安 105 | ああ　*ā*　ah, oh |

あ（stroke order 1,2,3）

あ　あ　あ

あ　あ　あ

| い *i* | 以 86 | いい　*ii*　good, alright　　　あい　*ai*　love, affection |

い（stroke order 1,2）

い　い　い

い　い　い

う u	宇 837	あう *au* meet		いう *iu* say

え e	衣 737	え *e* picture, painting / うえ *ue* top, area above		ええ *ē* yes, yeah, uh-huh / いいえ *iie* no

お o	於 2048	あおい *aoi* blue, green	おおい *ōi* lots of, many

お お お

お お お

か ka	加 496	かお *kao* face あかい *akai* red	かう *kau* buy, purchase えいが *eiga* movie

か か か

か か か

き ki	幾 534	あき *aki* autumn おおきい *ōkii* big, large	えき *eki* (train) staition かぎ *kagi* key

き

| き | き | き | | | | |

| | | | | | | |

| | | | | | | |

き	き	き											

く ku	久 896	いく *iku* go かく *kaku* write	きく *kiku* hear, ask かぐ *kagu* furniture

く

| く | く | く | | | | |

| | | | | | | |

| | | | | | | |

く	く	く											

| け ke | 計 190 | いけ　*ike*　pond | | けいかく　*keikaku*　plan, project |

け　け　け

け　け　け

| こ ko | 己 1006 | ここ　*koko*　here, this place
ごご　*gogo*　afternoon | | こえ　*koe*　voice
えいご　*eigo*　English (language) |

こ　こ　こ

こ　こ　こ

さ *sa*	左 55	さあ *sā* well now, alright	あさ *asa* morning
		さけ *sake* saké	けいざい *keizai* economy

さ　さ　さ

さ　さ　さ

し *shi*	之 1980	あし *ashi* leg, foot	いし *ishi* stone
		おいしい *oishii* tasty, tastes good	あじ *aji* taste, savor

し　し　し

し　し　し

す su	寸 1923	すし *sushi* sushi		あす *asu* tomorrow
		いす *isu* chair		かず *kazu* number

せ se	世 163	あせ *ase* sweat, perspiration		せかい *sekai* world
		かぜ *kaze* wind, breeze		せいじ *seiji* politics

そ *so*	曽 –	そう　*sō*　so, like that うそ　*uso*　lie, falsehood	そこ　*soko*　there かぞく　*kazoku*　family

そ　そ　そ

そ　そ　そ

た *ta*	太 466	たかい　*takai*　high; expensive かた　*kata*　person (polite); shoulder	した　*shita*　bottom, area below ただしい　*tadashii*　correct

た　た　た

た　た　た

ち *chi*	知 147	ちいさい *chiisai* little, small いち *ichi* one	ちかい *chikai* near うち *uchi* home, residence

ち ち ち

ち ち ち

つ *tsu*	川 30	つぎ *tsugi* the next いくつ *ikutsu* how many	つかう *tsukau* use がっこう *gakkō* school

つ つ つ

つ つ つ

て *te*	天 73	て　*te*　hand　　　　　　　　　ちかてつ　*chikatetsu*　subway
		きって　*kitte*　(postage) stamp　　です　*desu*　be

| ¹て | て | て | て | | | | | | |

| て | て | て |

と *to*	止 228	とおい　*tōi*　far　　　　　　　　　とし　*toshi*　year; city
		せいと　*seito*　pupil, student　　いちど　*ichido*　one time, once

| ¹と² | と | と | と | | | | | | |

| と | と | と |

な na	奈 1173	ななつ *nanatsu* seven なか *naka* the inside	なつ *natsu* summer おなじ *onaji* the same

な　な　な

な　な　な

に ni	仁 1660	にし *nishi* west にど *nido* twice, two times	にく *niku* meat なに *nani* what

に　に　に

に　に　に

21

| ぬ nu | 奴 1959 | ぬぐ *nugu* take/peel off | | いぬ *inu* dog |
| しぬ *shinu* die | | | | きぬ *kinu* silk |

ぬ　ぬ　ぬ

ぬ　ぬ　ぬ

| ね ne | 祢 – | ねこ *neko* cat | | ねがい *negai* a request |
| おかね *okane* money | | | | あね *ane* elder sister |

ね　ね　ね

ね　ね　ね

の *no*	乃 1979	のて　　*node*　because, since	のど　*nodo*　throat
		この　　*kono*　this	たのしい　*tanoshii*　merry, pleasant

の

の　の　の

の　の　の

は *ha/wa*	波 732	はは（は）　*haha (wa)*　mother (*wa* = particle)　はい　*hai*　yes
		にばい　*nibai*　double, twice as much　　しっぱい　*shippai*　failure, flop

は

は　は　は

は　は　は

ひ *hi*	比 777	ひと *hito* person, man				ひがし *higashi* east			
		くび *kubi* neck				いっぴき *ippiki* one (animal)			

¹ひ

	ひ	ひ	ひ						

ひ	ひ	ひ												

ふ *fu*	不 100	ふたつ *futatsu* two				ふね *fune* ship			
		どうぶつ *dōbutsu* animal				きっぷ *kippu* ticket			

¹³²⁴ふ

	ふ	ふ	ふ						

ふ	ふ	ふ												

| へ he/e | 部 254 | へた　*heta*　unskillfulness
かべ　*kabe*　wall | どこへ　*doko e*　where to
ぺらぺら　*perapera*　(speak) fluently |

へ

| へ | へ | へ |

| へ | へ | へ |

| ほ *ho* | 保 1026 | ほか　*hoka*　other
ぼうし　*bōshi*　hat | ほね　*hone*　bone
ぽかぽか　*pokapoka*　repeatedly |

ほ

| ほ | ほ | ほ |

| ほ | ほ | ほ |

| ま ma | 末 330 | まつ *matsu* wait | | なまえ *namae* name | |
| | | しま *shima* island | | いま *ima* now | |

ま ま ま

ま ま ま

| み mi | 美 375 | みみ *mimi* ear | | みせ *mise* shop, store | |
| | | うみ *umi* sea, ocean | | みなみ *minami* south |

み み み

み み み

| む mu | 武 846 | むっつ *muttsu* six
のむ *nomu* drink | | | | むずかしい *muzukashii* difficult
さむい *samui* cold | | |

む

む む む

む む む

| め me | 女 62 | めいし *meishi* name card
だめ *dame* useless, vain | | | | あめ *ame* rain
いつつめ *itsutsume* the fifth | | |

め

め め め

め め め

| も mo | 毛 643 | もの *mono* thing, object | もう *mō* already |
| | | もじ *moji* character, letter | もっと *motto* more |

も　も　も

も　も　も

| や ya | 也 1981 | やすい *yasui* cheap, inexpensive | やさしい *yasashii* easy, simple |
| | | やま *yama* mountain | ひゃく *hyaku* hundred |

や　や　や

や　や　や

ゆ *yu*	由 356	ゆき *yuki* snow ふゆ *fuyu* winter	ゆうめい *yūmei* famous きゅう *kyū* nine

ゆ ゆ ゆ

ゆ ゆ ゆ

よ *yo*	与 429	よい *yoi* good, alright よっつ *yottsu* four	よむ *yomu* read きょう *kyō* today

よ よ よ

よ よ よ

ら ra	良 339	から　*kara*　from; because ひらがな　*hiragana*　hiragana	いくら　*ikura*　how much さようなら　*sayōnara*　goodbye

ら　ら　ら

ら　ら　ら

り ri	利 342	かなり　*kanari*　quite, rather まつり　*matsuri*　festival	あります　*arimasu*　be (present) りょこう　*ryokō*　trip, travel

り　り　り

り　り　り

| る ru | 留 514 | くる *kuru* come | ある *aru* be |
| | | よる *yoru* (at) night, evening | ふるい *furui* old |

| れ re | 礼 462 | れい *rei* example | これ *kore* this |
| | | かれ *kare* he | きれい *kirei* pretty; clean |

| ろ *ro* | 呂 1415 | ろく *roku* six | | | | いろ *iro* color | | |
| | | しろい *shiroi* white | | | | ところ *tokoro* place | | |

ろ

| ろ | ろ | ろ | | | | | | |
| | | | | | | | | |

| | | | | | | | | |
| | | | | | | | | |

ろ	ろ	ろ											

| わ *wa* | 和 263 | わたし *watashi* I | | | | わかる *wakaru* understand | | |
| | | わるい *warui* bad, evil | | | | にわ には *niwa ni wa* in the garden | | |

わ

| わ | わ | わ | | | | | | |
| | | | | | | | | |

| | | | | | | | | |
| | | | | | | | | |

わ	わ	わ											

| を o | 遠 395 | おちゃ を のむ *ocha o nomu* drink (green) tea
しお を かう *shio o kau* buy salt |

を を を

を を を

| ん n | 尤 – | なん *nan* what   よん *yon* four
おんな *onna* woman   かんぱい *Kanpai!* To your health! |

ん ん ん

ん ん ん

ア *a*	阿 2198	アー *aa* ah, oh

1 ア **2**	ア	ア	ア				

ア	ア	ア									

イ *i*	伊 1987	イー *ii* good, alright	アイ *ai* love, affection

イ **1** **2**	イ	イ	イ				

イ	イ	イ									

ウ *u*	宇 837	アウ *au* meet	イウ *iu* say

ウ ウ ウ

ウ ウ ウ

エ *e*	江 1121	エ *e* picture, painting ウエ *ue* top, area above	エー *ee* yes, yeah, uh-huh イーエ *iie* no

エ エ エ

エ エ エ

オ o	於 2048	アオイ *aoi* blue, green			オーイ *ooi* lots of, many		

才 (1, 2, 3)

才	才	才					

オ	オ	オ												

カ ka	加 496	カー *kā* car					

力 (1, 2)

力	力	力					

力	力	力												

キ *ki*	幾 534	キー　*kī*　key

キ　キ　キ

キ　キ　キ

ク *ku*	久 896	アーク　*āku*　(electric) arc

ク　ク　ク

ク　ク　ク

ケ ke	箇 1536	ケーキ *kēki* cake	オーケー *ōkē* O.K., okay

ケ ケ ケ

ケ ケ ケ

コ ko	己 1006	コア *koa* core	ゴア *Goa* Goa

コ コ コ

コ コ コ

サ *sa*	散 516	サー　*sā*　sir

サ　サ　サ

サ　サ　サ

シ *shi*	之 1980	シガー　*shigā*　cigar	アジア　*ajia*　Asia

シ　シ　シ

シ　シ　シ

| ス *su* | 須 1512 | スキー *sukī* skiing, skis | ガス *gasu* gas |
| | | コース *kōsu* course | スイス *Suisu* Switzerland |

ス

| ス | ス | ス | | | | | |
| | | | | | | | |

| | | | | | | | | |
| | | | | | | | | |

ス	ス	ス								

| セ *se* | 世 163 | セクシー *sekushī* sexy | ガーゼ *gāze* gauze |

セ

| セ | セ | セ | | | | | |
| | | | | | | | |

| | | | | | | | | |
| | | | | | | | | |

セ	セ	セ								

ソ so	曽 –	ソース　*sōsu*　sauce			ソーセージ　*sōsēji*　sausage				
ソ	ソ	ソ	ソ	ソ					
ソ ソ ソ									

タ ta	多 154	タクシー　*takushī*　taxi　　ギター　*gitā*　guitar			ウエーター　*uētā*　waiter　　えいがスター　*eiga sutā*　movie star				
タ	タ	タ	タ	タ					
タ タ タ									

チ chi	千	15	チーズ *chīzu* cheese			チェス *chesu* chess			
			チ	チ	チ				
チ	チ	チ							

ツ tsu	川	30	スーツケース *sūtsukēsu* suitcase サッカー *sakkā* soccer			クッキー *kukkī* cookie チェック *chekku* check			
			ツ	ツ	ツ				
ツ	ツ	ツ							

| テ *te* | 天 73 | データ *dēta* data　　　　　　　ディスク *disuku* disk
シーディー *shīdī* CD (compact disk) |

テ　テ　テ

テ　テ　テ

| ト *to* | 止 228 | テスト *tesuto* test　　　　　　テキスト *tekisuto* text
スカート *sukāto* skirt　　　　　ドット *dotto* dot |

ト　ト　ト

ト　ト　ト

| ナ na | 奈 1173 | ナチ（ス）　*nachi(su)*　the Nazis | | カナダ　*Kanada*　Canada |

ナ ナ ナ ナ

ナ ナ ナ

| ニ ni | 仁 1660 | ニーズ　*nīzu*　needs | | テニス　*tenisu*　tennis |

二 二 二 二

二 二 二

| ヌ *nu* | 奴 1959 | ヌード *nūdo* nude | カヌー *kanū* canoe |

ヌ ヌ ヌ

ヌ ヌ ヌ

| ネ *ne* | 祢 – | ネクタイ *nekutai* necktie　　ゼネスト *zenesuto* general strike
ネガ *nega* (photographic) negative |

ネ ネ ネ

ネ ネ ネ

| ノ no | 乃 1979 | ノー *nō* no | ノート *nōto* notebook |

ノ¹ ノ ノ ノ

ノ ノ ノ

| ハ ha | 八 10 | バス *basu* bus | バナナ *banana* banana |
| | | スーパー *sūpā* supermarket | デパート *depāto* department store |

ハ ハ ハ

ハ ハ ハ

ヒ *hi*	比 777	コーヒー	*kōhī*	coffee		ビデオ	*bideo*	video
		サービス	*sābisu*	service		コピー	*kopī*	copy

²ヒ¹

ヒ ヒ ヒ

ヒ ヒ ヒ

フ *fu*	不 100	ナイフ	*naifu*	knife		ストーブ	*sutōbu*	stove
		コップ	*koppu*	(drinking) glass		フォーク	*fōku*	fork

¹フ

フ フ フ

フ フ フ

へ he	部 254	ベッド　*beddo*　bed ページ　*pēji*　page				データーベース　*dētābēsu*　database				

へ

ホ ho	保 1026	ホステス　*hosutesu*　hostess ポスト　*posuto*　post(box)				ボーナス　*bōnasu*　bonus スポーツ　*supōtsu*　sports				

ホ

マ *ma*	末 330	ママ *mama* mama テーマ *tēma* theme			パーマ *pāma* permanent (wave) マーケット *māketto* market			
マ		マ	マ	マ				

マ	マ	マ												

ミ *mi*	三 4	ミニカー *minikā* minicar マスコミ *masukomi* mass communication			ミス *misu* mistake; Miss ゼミ *zemi* seminar			
ミ		ミ	ミ	ミ				

ミ	ミ	ミ												

ム mu	牟 －	ゲーム *gēmu* game	ブーム *būmu* boom
		ハム *hamu* ham	けしゴム *keshigomu* eraser

ム　ム　ム

ム　ム　ム

メ me	女 62	メーデー *mēdē* May Day	メッセージ *messēji* message
		メキシコ *Mekishiko* Mexico	メッカ *Mekka* Mecca

メ　メ　メ

メ　メ　メ

モ mo	毛 643	モーター *mōtā* motor メモ *memo* memo, note, list	モットー *mottō* motto デモ *demo* demonstration

モ モ モ

モ モ モ

ヤ ya	也 1981	カヤック *kayakku* kayak シャツ *shatsu* undershirt	ジャズ *jazu* jazz キャベツ *kyabetsu* cabbage

ヤ ヤ ヤ

ヤ ヤ ヤ

ユ yu	由 356	ユニーク *yunīku* unique		ユーモア *yūmoa* humor
		ニュース *nyūsu* news		メニュー *menyū* menu

ユ ユ ユ

ユ ユ ユ

ヨ yo	與 -	ヨット *yotto* yacht	ニューヨーク *Nyū Yōku* New York
		ショー *shō* show	

ヨ ヨ ヨ

ヨ ヨ ヨ

| ラ ra | 良 339 | ラジオ *rajio* radio
カラー *karā* color | | | カメラ *kamera* camera
グラム *guramu* gram | | |

ラ ラ ラ

| リ ri | 利 342 | リズム *rizumu* rhythm
ミリ *miri* millimeter | | | リスト *risuto* list
ベーカリー *bēkarī* bakery | | |

リ リ リ

ル ru	流 304	ビル *biru* building ホテル *hoteru* hotel	ビール *bīru* beer ドル *doru* dollar

ル ル ル

ル ル ル

レ re	礼 462	レコード *rekōdo* record トイレ *toire* toilet	ステレオ *sutereo* stereo エレベーター *erebētā* elevator

レ レ レ

レ レ レ

| 口 *ro* | 呂 1415 | ロビー | *robī* | lobby | | | ローマじ | *rōmaji* | roman letters | |
| | | ロシア | *Roshia* | Russia | | | ゼロ | *zero* | zero | |

口

ロ ロ ロ

| 口 | 口 | 口 | | | | | | | | | | |

| ワ *wa* | 和 263 | ワープロ | *wāpuro* | word processor | | | ワイシャツ | *waishatsu* | shirt | |
| | | タワー | *tawā* | tower | | | シャワー | *shawā* | shower | |

ワ

ワ ワ ワ

| ワ | ワ | ワ | | | | | | | | | | |

| ヲ o | 乎 – | シャワー ヲ アビル　*shawā o abiru*　take a shower |

ヲ ヲ ヲ

ヲ ヲ ヲ

| ン n | 尓 – | センター　*sentā*　center | ワイン　*wain*　wine |
| | | パーセント　*pāsento*　percent | コンピュータ　*konpyūta*　computer |

ン ン ン

ン ン ン

1	イ 2a/3	***JIN, NIN, hito*** – human being, man, person

アメリカ人   *Amerikajin*   an American
１００人   *hyakunin*   100 people
５、６人   *go-rokunin*   5 or 6 people
あの人   *ano hito*   that person, he, she

人   人 人 人

2	－ / 一 0a/1	***ICHI, ITSU, hito(tsu), hito-*** – one

一ページ   *ichi pēji*   one page; page 1
一々   *ichi-ichi*   one by one; in full detail
一つ一つ   *hitotsu-hitotsu*   one by one, individually
一人   *hitori*   one person; alone   1

一   一 一 一

3	‐/二 0a/4	**NI, futa(tsu), futa-** – two

二人　　*futari, ninin*　two people ... 1
一人二人　*hitori-futari*　one or two people ... 2, 1, 1
二人ずつ　*futarizutsu*　two by two, every two people ... 1
二つずつ　*futatsuzutsu*　two by two, two at a time

4	‐ 二 一 0a 4 1	**SAN, mit(tsu), mi(tsu), mi-** – three

三人　*sannin*　three people ... 1
二、三人　*ni-sannin*　two or three people ... 3, 1
三キロ　*san kiro*　3 kg; 3 km
三つぞろい　*mitsuzoroi*　three-piece suit

5	日 4c/42	**NICHI, JITSU, hi, -ka** – day; sun; (short for) Japan	

一 日　*ichinichi, ichijitsu*　one day　　2
一 日　*tsuitachi*　1st of the month　　2
二 日　*futsuka*　two days; 2nd of the month　　3
三 日　*mikka*　three days; 3rd of the month　　4

6	口 儿 3s/24　16	**SHI, yot(tsu), yo(tsu), yo-, yon** – four	

四 人　*yonin*　four people　　1
四 日　*yokka*　four days; 4th of the month　　5
三、四日　*san-yokka*　three or four days　　4, 5
三、四人　*san-yonin*　three or four people　　4, 1

7	– 一 一 0a 14 1	***GO, itsu(tsu), itsu-*** – five	
		五人　*gonin*　five people	1
		五日　*itsuka*　five days; 5th of the month	5
		四、五日　*shi-gonichi*　four or five days	6, 5
		四、五人　*shi-gonin*　four or five people	6, 1

五　五　五

五　五　五

8	亠 儿 2j/11 16	***ROKU, mut(tsu), mu(tsu), mu-, [mui-]*** – six	
		六人　*rokunin*　six people	1
		五、六人　*go-rokunin*　five or six people	7, 1
		六日　*muika*　six days; 6th of the month	5
		五、六日　*go-rokunichi*　five or six days	7, 5

六　六　六

六　六　六

9	– / 十 0a/12	**SHICHI, nana(tsu), nana-, [nano-]** – seven

七人　*shichinin*　seven people　　　　　　　　　　　　　　　　1
七日　*nanoka*　seven days; 7th of the month　　　　　　　　　5
七メートル　*nana mētoru, shichi mētoru*　7 m
七五三　*shichi-go-san*　festival day for 3-, 5-, and 7-year-olds (Nov. 15)　7, 4

10	ˇ 2o/16	**HACHI, yat(tsu), ya(tsu), ya-, [yō-]** – eight

八人　*hachinin*　eight people　　　　　　　　　　　　　　　　1
八日　*yōka*　eight days; 8th of the month　　　　　　　　　　5
八ミリ　*hachi miri*　8 mm
八グラム　*hachi guramu*　8 grams

11	−/十 0a/12

KYŪ, KU, kokono(tsu), kokono- – nine

九人　*kyūnin, kunin*　nine people　　1
九日　*kokonoka*　nine days; 9th of the month　　5
九ドル　*kyū doru*　nine dollars
九ユーロ　*kyū yūro*　nine euro(s)

九 九 九

九 九 九

12	十 2k/12

JŪ, JI', tō, to- – ten

十人　*jūnin*　ten people　　1
十日　*tōka*　ten days; 10th of the month　　5
二十日　*hatsuka*　20 days; 20th of the month　　3, 5
十四日　*jūyokka*　14 days; 14th of the month　　6, 5

十 十 十

十 十 十

13	冂 冖 2r/20 11	**EN** – circle; yen **maru(i)** – round
		一円　*ichi en*　one yen　2
		二円　*ni en*　two yen　3
		三円　*san en*　three yen　4
		四円　*yo en*　four yen　6

14	日 一 4c/42 14	**HYAKU** – hundred
		百人　*hyakunin*　100 people　1
		八百円　*happyaku en*　800 yen　10, 13
		九百　*kyūhyaku*　900　11
		三百六十五日　*sanbyaku rokujūgonichi*　365 days　4, 8, 12, 7, 5

15	千 丨 2k/12 2	**SEN, chi** – thousand									
		一千　　*issen*　1,000									2
		三千　　*sanzen*　3,000									4
		八千　　*hassen*　8,000									10
		千円　　*sen en*　1,000 yen									13

千

千　千　千

千　千　千

16	一 丆 一 0a 14 1	**MAN** – ten thousand **BAN** – many, all									
		一万円　　*ichiman en*　10,000 yen									2, 13
		百万　　*hyakuman*　1 million									14
		一千万円　　*issenman en*　10 million yen									2, 15, 13
		二、三万円　　*ni-sanman en*　20,000-30,000 yen									3, 4, 13

万

万　万　万

万　万　万

17	月 4b/43	**GETSU, tsuki** – moon; month **GATSU** – month

一月　*ichigatsu*　January　　　　　　　　　　　　　　　　2
一月　*hitotsuki*　one month　　　　　　　　　　　　　　2
一か月　*ikkagetsu*　one month　　　　　　　　　　　　　2
一月八日＝１月８日　*ichigatsu yōka*　January 8　　　　2, 10, 5, 5

月　月　月　月

月　月　月

18	火 4d/44	**KA, hi, [ho]** – fire

９月４日（火）　*kugatsu yokka (ka)*　(Tuesday) September 4　　　17, 5

火　火　火

火　火　火

19	⺡ 3a/21	***SUI, mizu*** – water

水火　*suika*　water and fire
水がめ　*mizugame*　water jug/jar
水かさ　*mizukasa*　volume of water (of a river)

18

水　水　水

水　水　水

20	木 4a/41	***BOKU, MOKU, ki, [ko]*** – tree; wood

三木　*Miki*　(surname)　　4
八木　*Yagi*　(surname)　　10

木　木　木

木　木　木

21	金 8a/72	**KIN, KON** – gold; metal; money **kane** – money **[kana]** – metal

月・水・金　*ges-sui-kin*　Monday, Wednesday, Friday   17, 19
金メダル　*kinmedaru*　gold medal
金ぱく　*kinpaku*　gold leaf/foil
金もうけ　*kanemōke*　making money

金　金　金

金　金　金

22	土 3b/22	**DO, TO, tsuchi** – earth, soil, ground

土木　*doboku*　civil engineering   20
土人　*dojin*　native, aborigine   1
土のう　*donō*　sandbag

土　土　土

土　土　土

| 23 | 一 十 一
 0a 41 1 | **HON** – book; origin; main; this; (counter for long, thin objects) **moto** – origin |

日本　*Nihon, Nippon*　Japan　　　　　　　　　　　　　5
日本人　*Nihonjin, Nipponjin*　a Japanese　　　　　5, 1
本日　*honjitsu*　today　　　　　　　　　　　　　　5
ビール六本　*bīru roppon*　six bottles of beer　　　　8

| 24 | – / 大
 0a/34 | **DAI, TAI, ō(kii), ō-** – big, large　**ō(i ni)** – very much, greatly |

大金　*taikin*　large amount of money　　　　　　21
大きさ　*ōkisa*　size
大水　*ōmizu*　flooding, overflow　　　　　　　　19
大みそか　*ōmisoka*　New Year's Eve

25	ʼʼ 3n/35	**SHŌ, chii(sai), ko-, o-** – little, small

小人 *kobito* dwarf, midget — 1
小人 *shōjin* insignificant person; small-minded man — 1
小人 *shōnin* child — 1
大小 *daishō* large and small; size — 24

26	一 ∥ │ 0a 24 2	**CHŪ** – middle; (short for) China **-CHŪ, -JŪ** – throughout, during, within **naka** – inside, midst

日本中 *Nihonjū, Nipponjū* all over Japan — 5, 23
一日中 *ichinichijū* all day long — 2, 5
日中 *nitchū* during the daytime — 5
日中 *Nit-Chū* Japanese-Chinese, Sino-Japanese — 5

27	雨 8d/74	***U, ame, [ama]*** – rain

大雨　　*ōame*　heavy rain, downpour　　24
小雨　　*kosame*　light rain, fine rain　　25
雨水　　*amamizu*　rainwater　　19
にわか雨　*niwakaame*　sudden shower

雨　雨　雨

雨　雨　雨

28	下 2m 14 2	***KA, GE, shita, moto*** – lower, base ***shimo*** – lower part ***sa(geru), o(rosu), kuda(su)*** – lower, hand down (a verdict) ***sa(garu)*** – hang down, fall ***o(riru)*** – get out of, get off (a vehicle) ***kuda(ru)*** – go/come down ***kuda(saru)*** – give

下水　　*gesui*　sewer system, drainage　　19
木下　　*Kinoshita*　(surname)　　20

下　下　下

下　下　下

| 29 | ┠ ㅡ 2m/13 1 | **JŌ, [SHŌ], ue** – upper **kami, [uwa-]** – upper part **a(geru)** – raise **a(garu), nobo(ru)** – rise **nobo(seru), nobo(su)** – bring up (a topic) |

水上　*suijō*　on the water　　　　　　　　　　　　　　　　19
上下　*jōge*　high and low, rise and fall; [volume] 1.2　　28
上り下り　*nobori-kudari*　ascent and descent, ups and downs　28

上　上　上

上　上　上

| 30 | ㅡ 儿 丨 0a 16 2 | **SEN, kawa** – river |

川上　*kawakami*　upstream; Kawakami (surname)　　　　29
川下　*kawashimo*　downstream　　　　　　　　　　　　28
小川　*ogawa*　stream, brook, creek; Ogawa (surname)　　25
ミシシッピー川　*Mishishippi-gawa*　Mississippi River

川　川　川

川　川　川

31	山 3o/36	**SAN, yama** – mountain

山水	*sansui*	landscape, natural scenery	19
火山	*kazan*	volcano	18
下山	*gezan*	descent from a mountain	28
山々	*yamayama*	mountains	

山　山　山

山　山　山

32	ハ 力 2o/16　8	**BUN** – portion **BU** – portion, 1 percent **FUN** – minute (of time/arc) **wa(keru), wa(katsu)** – divide, share, distinguish **wa(kareru)** – be separated **wa(karu)** – understand

十分	*jūbun*	enough, sufficient, adequate	12
十分	*jippun, juppun*	10 minutes	12
十分の一	*jūbun no ichi*	one tenth, 10 percent	12, 2

分　分　分

分　分　分

33	口 王 丶
	3s/24 46 2

KOKU, kuni – country

大国	*taikoku*	large country, major power	24
万国	*bankoku*	all countries, world	16
四国	*Shikoku*	(one of the 4 main islands of Japan)	6
中国	*Chūgoku*	China; (region in western Honshū)	26

国

国 国 国

国 国 国

34	日 土 寸
	4c/42 22 37

JI, toki – time; hour

四時二十分＝４時２０分	*yoji nijippun, yoji nijuppun*	4:20	6, 3, 12, 32
一時	*ichiji*	for a time; 1 o'clock	2
一時	*hitotoki, ittoki*	a while, moment	2
時々	*tokidoki*	sometimes	

時

時 時 時

時 時 時

35	門 日 8e/75　42	**KAN, KEN, aida** – interval (between)　**ma** – interval (between); a room

時間　*jikan*　time; hour　　　　　　　　　　　　　　　　　　　34
中間　*chūkan*　middle, intermediate　　　　　　　　　　　　　26
人間　*ningen*　human being　　　　　　　　　　　　　　　　　1
間もなく　*mamonaku*　presently, in a little while, soon

間　間　間

間　間　間

36	一 土 ⺊ 0a　22　15	**SEI, SHŌ** – life　**i(kiru), i(keru)** – be alive　**i(kasu)** – revive, bring to life　**u(mu)** – bear (a child) / be born　**u(mareru)** – grow　**ha(yasu), ha(eru), o(u)** – raw, draft (beer)　**nama** – raw　**ki-** – pure

人生　*jinsei*　life, human life　　　　　　　　　　　　　　　　1
一生　*isshō*　one's whole life　　　　　　　　　　　　　　　　2

生　生　生

生　生　生

37   0a   15   12

NEN, toshi – year

生年月日   *seinengappi*   date of birth   36, 17, 5
三年生   *sannensei*   third-year student, junior   4, 36
五年間   *gonenkan*   for 5 years   7, 35
年金   *nenkin*   pension, annuity   21

38   2o/16   43   8

ZEN, mae – before, in front of, earlier

前もって   *maemotte*   beforehand, in advance
人前（で）   *hitomae (de)*   before others, in public   1
分け前   *wakemae*   one's share   32
二人前   *nininmae, futarimae*   enough for two people   3, 1

39	彳 攵 厶 3i/29　49　17	**GO, nochi** – after, later **KŌ, ushi(ro)** – behind **ato** – afterward, subsequent, back **oku(reru)** – be late, ⌐lag behind

後

前後　　zengo　　approximately; front and rear　　　　　　　　　　　38
後日　　gojitsu　　the future, another day　　　　　　　　　　　　　5
その後　　sono go　　thereafter, later
後年　　kōnen　　in later/future years, afterward　　　　　　　　37

40	十 ノ一 2k/12　15	**GO** – noon

午

午前　　gozen　　morning, a.m.　　　　　　　　　　　　　　　38
午後　　gogo　　afternoon, p.m.　　　　　　　　　　　　　　　39
午前中　　gozenchū　　all morning, before noon　　　　　　　38, 26
午後四時　　gogo yoji　　4:00 p.m.　　　　　　　　　　　39, 6, 34

41	土 儿 丨 3b/22 16 2	**SEN, saki** – earlier; ahead; priority; future; destination; the tip

先日　senjitsu　recently, the other day　　5
先月　sengetsu　last month　　17
先々月　sensengetsu　month before last　　17
先生　sensei　teacher　　36

42	亻 一 2a/3 1	**KON, KIN, ima** – now

今日　konnichi, kyō　today　　5
今月　kongetsu　this month　　17
今年　kotoshi　this year　　37
今後　kongo　after this, from now on　　39

43	−ノ入 0a/3	***NYŪ, hai(ru), i(ru)*** – go/come/get in, enter ***i(reru)*** – put/let in

入国   *nyūkoku*   entry (into a country)   33
金入れ   *kaneire*   cashbox; purse, wallet   21
日の入り   *hi no iri*   sunset   5
入り日   *irihi*   setting sun   5

44	− 出 冂 0a 36 20	***SHUTSU, [SUI], da(su)*** – take out; send ***de(ru)*** – go/come out

出火   *shukka*   outbreak of fire   18
出入り   *deiri*   coming and going (of people)   43
人出   *hitode*   turnout, crowds   1
日の出   *hi no de*   sunrise   5

45 | イ 木
2a/3 41

KYŪ, yasu(mu) – rest; take the day off **yasu(meru)** – give it a rest **yasu(maru)** – be rested

休日	kyūjitsu	holiday, day off	5
休火山	kyūkazan	nonactive volcano	18, 31
一休み	hitoyasumi	short rest; a break, recess	2
中休み	nakayasumi	take a break	26

休

休 休 休

休 休 休

46 | 目 貝
5c 68

KEN, mi(ru) – see **mi(eru)** – be visible **mi(seru)** – show

一見	ikken	(quick) glance	2
先見	senken	foresight	41
見本	mihon	sample (of merchandise)	23
見出し	midashi	heading, headline	44

見

見 見 見

見 見 見

47	門 耳 8e/75　65	**BUN, MON, ki(ku)** – hear, heed; ask **ki(koeru)** – be audible
		見聞　*kenbun*　information, observation　　　　　　　　　　　46
		聞き入れる　*kikiireru*　comply with　　　　　　　　　　　43

聞

48	言 口 一 7a/67　24　14	**GO** – word **kata(ru)** – talk, relate **kata(rau)** – converse
		日本語　*nihongo*　Japanese language　　　　　　　　　　　5, 23
		国語　*kokugo*　national/Japanese language　　　　　　　　　33
		中国語　*chūgokugo*　Chinese language　　　　　　　　　26, 33
		見出し語　*midashigo*　headword, entry word　　　　　　46, 44

語

49	彳 二 丨
	3i/29　4　2

KŌ, [AN], i(ku), yu(ku) – go **GYŌ** – line (of text) **okona(u)** – do, perform, carry out

一行	ikkō	party, retinue	2
一行	ichigyō	a line (of text)	2
行間	gyōkan	space between lines (of text)	35
行き先	ikisaki, yukisaki	destination	41

50	一 米 一
	0a　62　1

RAI, ku(ru), kita(ru) – come **kita(su)** – bring about

来年	rainen	next year	37
来月	raigetsu	next month	17
来日	rainichi	come to Japan	5
本来	honrai	originally, primarily	23

51	一 木 日 0a 41 42	**TŌ, higashi** – east

中東　*Chūtō*　Middle East　　26
東大　*Tōdai*　Tokyo University (short for Tōkyō Daigaku)　24
東アジア　*Higashi-Ajia*　East Asia
東ヨーロッパ　*Higashi-Yōroppa*　East Europe

東　東　東

東　東　東

52	一 刀 一 0a 24 14	**SEI, SAI, nishi** – west; (SEI = short for) Spain

東西　*tōzai*　east and west　　51
西日本　*Nishi Nihon*　western Japan　　5, 23
西ヨーロッパ　*Nishi-Yōroppa*　Western Europe
西日　*nishibi*　the afternoon sun　　5

西　西　西

西　西　西

53	一 ┣ 一 0a 13 1	**HOKU, kita** – north

北

東北 *Tōhoku* (region in northern Honshū) — 51
北東 *hokutō* northeast — 51
北北東 *hokuhokutō* north-northeast — 51
北川 *Kitagawa* (surname) — 30

北 北 北

北 北 北

54	十 冂 儿 2k/12 20 16	**NAN, [NA], minami** – south

南

西南 *seinan* southwest — 52
東南アジア *Tōnan-Ajia* Southeast Asia — 51
南北 *nanboku* south and north, north-south — 53
南アルプス *Minami-Arupusu* Southern (Japan) Alps

南 南 南

南 南 南

55	一 工 十
	0a 38 12

SA, hidari – left

左上　*hidariue*　upper left　29
左下　*hidarishita*　lower left　28

左　左　左

左　左　左

56	凵 十
	3d/24 12

U, YŪ, migi – right

左右　*sayū*　left and right; control　55
右上　*migi ue*　upper right　29
右下　*migi shita*　lower right　28
右から左へ　*migi kara hidari e*　from right to left; quickly　55

右　右　右

右　右　右

57	ﾛ ﾀ 3d/24　30	***MEI, MYŌ, na*** – name; reputation	
		人名　*jinmei*　name of a person	1
		名人　*meijin*　master, expert, virtuoso	1
		大名　*daimyō*　(Japanese) feudal lord	24
		名前　*namae*　a name	38

名

58	ﾄ ﾀ 2m/13　30	***GAI, GE, soto*** – outside ***hoka*** – other ***hazu(reru), hazu(su)*** – slip off, miss	
		外国　*gaikoku*　foreign country	33
		外（国）人　*gai(koku)jin*　foreigner	33, 1
		外来語　*gairaigo*　word of foreign origin, loanword	50, 48
		外出　*gaishutsu*　go out	44

外

59	一 十 儿 0a 12 16	**HAN, naka(ba)** – half

半分　*hanbun*　half　　　　　　　　　　　　　　　32
半年　*hantoshi*　half a year, 6 months　　　　　37
三時半　*sanji han*　half past three, 3:30　　　　4, 34
前半　*zenhan, zenpan*　first half　　　　　　　38

半　半　半

半　半　半

60	一 ᶓ ┣ 0a 57 13	**CHŌ** – long; chief, head **naga(i)** – long

長時間　*chōjikan*　long time, many hours　　　34, 35
長円　*chōen*　ellipse, oval　　　　　　　　　　13
長年　*naganen*　many years, long years　　　　37
長い間　*nagai aida*　for a long time　　　　　35

長　長　長

長　長　長

61	甲 力 5f/58　8

DAN, NAN, otoko – man, human male

長男	chōnan	eldest son	60
男の人	otoko no hito	man	1
山男	yamaotoko	mountain dweller; mountaineer	31
大男	ōotoko	giant, tall man	24

男　男　男

男　男　男

62	女 3e/25

JO, NYO, [NYŌ], onna – woman **me** – feminine

長女	chōjo	eldest daughter	60
男女	danjo	men and women	61
女の人	onna no hito	woman	1
女中	jochū	maid	26

女　女　女

女　女　女

63	子 2c/6	**SHI, SU, ko** – child	
		男子　　*danshi*　boy, man	61
		男の子　*otoko no ko*　boy	61
		女子　　*joshi*　girl, woman	62
		女の子　*onna no ko*　girl	62

64	電 日 丨 8d/74　42　2	**DEN** – electricity	
		休電　　*kyūden*　electricity cut-off, power outage	45
		電子　　*denshi*　electron	63
		電子レンジ　*denshi renji*　microwave oven	63

65	⺍ 冂 子 3n/35 20 6	**GAKU** – science, study **mana(bu)** – learn	
		大学　*daigaku*　university, college	24
		入学　*nyūgaku*　entry/admission into a school	43
		学生　*gakusei*　student	36
		中学生　*chūgakusei*　junior-high-school student	26, 36

66	一 𫟃 乀 0a 25 2	**BO, haha** – mother	
		母子　*boshi*　mother and child	63
		生母　*seibo*　one's biological mother	36
		母国語　*bokokugo*　one's mother tongue	33, 48
		お母さん　*okāsan*　mother	

67	ᵛ 𣥂 2o/16 12	**FU, chichi** – father	
		父母　*fubo, chichihaha*　father and mother	66
		父子　*fushi*　father and child/son	63
		父上　*chichiue*　father (honorific)	29
		お父さん　*otōsan*　father	

父　父　父

父父父

68	木 宀 儿 4a/41 11 16	**KŌ** – school; (printing) proof	
		学校　*gakkō*　school	65
		小学校　*shōgakkō*　elementary school	25, 65
		中学校　*chūgakkō*　junior high school	26, 65
		校長　*kōchō*　principal, headmaster	60

校　校　校

校校校

69	一 ケ ケ
	0a 25 15

MAI – every, each

毎年	mainen, maitoshi	every year, annual	37
毎月	maigetsu, maitsuki	every month, monthly	17
毎日	mainichi	every day, daily	5
毎時	maiji	every hour, hourly, per hour	34

毎

毎 毎 毎

毎 毎 毎

70	日 土 ヨ
	4c/42 22 39

SHO, ka(ku) – write

書名	shomei	book title	57
前書き	maegaki	foreword, preface	38
下書き	shitagaki	rough draft	28
書き入れる	kakiireru	write/fill in, enter	43

書

書 書 書

書 書 書

71	車 7c/69	**SHA, kuruma** – vehicle; wheel	
		電車 *densha* electric train	64
		外車 *gaisha* foreign car	58
		下車 *gesha* get off (a train)	28
		水車 *suisha* waterwheel	19

72	一 仁 气 0a 15 12	**KI, KE** – spirit, soul, mood	
		人気 *ninki* popularity	1
		気分 *kibun* feeling, mood	32
		本気 *honki* seriousness, (in) earnest	23
		電気 *denki* electricity	64

73	一 大 一 0a 34 1	**TEN, ame, [ama]** – heaven

天気   *tenki*   weather   72
天国   *tengoku*   paradise   33
天の川   *Amanogawa*   Milky Way   30
天下   *tenka*   the whole country; the public/world   28

74	亠 口 冂 2j/11 24 20	**KŌ, taka(i)** – high; expensive **taka** – amount, quantity **taka(maru)** – rise **taka(meru)** – raise

高校   *kōkō*   senior high school (short for *kōtō gakkō*)   68
高校生   *kōkōsei*   senior-high-school student   68, 36
名高い   *nadakai*   renowned, famous   57
高木   *Takagi*   (surname)   20

75	日 丨 4c/42　2

HAKU, BYAKU, shiro(i), shiro, [shira] – white

白人	*hakujin*	a white, Caucasian	1
白書	*hakusho*	a white paper (on), report	70
白金	*hakkin*	platinum	21
白木	*shiraki*	plain/unpainted/unvarnished wood	20

白　白　白

白　白　白

76	言 日 十 7a/67　24　12

WA, hanashi – conversation, story **hana(su)** – speak

電話	*denwa*	telephone	64
話し中	*hanashichū*	in the midst of speaking; (phone is) busy	26

話　話　話

話　話　話

77	言 土 冂 7a/67 22 20	**DOKU, TOKU, [TŌ], yo(mu)** – read

読書　　*dokusho*　reading　　　　　　　　　　70
読本　　*tokuhon*　reader, book of readings　　23

78	又 十 2h/9 12	**YŪ, tomo** – friend

友人　　*yūjin*　friend　　　　　　　　　　　　　　1
学友　　*gakuyū*　fellow student, classmate; alumnus　65
校友　　*kōyū*　schoolmate, alumnus　　　　　　68

79 食 8b/77	**SHOKU, [JIKI]** – food, eating **ta(beru), ku(u), ku(rau)** – eat	
	一食　*isshoku*　a meal	2
	三食　*sanshoku*　three meals (a day)	4
	人食い　*hitokui*　man-eating, cannibalism	1

80 2a/3 24 14	**KA, nani, [nan]** – what, which, how many	
	何時　*nanji*　what time	34
	何時間　*nanjikan*　how many hours	34, 35
	何日　*nannichi*　how many days; what day of the month	5
	何人　*nannin*　how many people	1

| 81 | 日 月 4c/42 43 | **MEI, a(kari)** – light, clearness **aka(rui), aki(raka)** – bright, clear **a(keru), aka(rumu), aka(ramu)** – become light **a(ku)** – be open **a(kasu)** – pass (the night) **a(kuru)** – next, following **MYŌ** – light; next |

明

明日　*myōnichi, asu*　tomorrow　5
明くる日　*akuru hi*　the next/following day　5

| 82 | 日 隹 彐 4c/42 73 39 | **YŌ** – day of the week |

曜

日曜日	*nichiyōbi*	Sunday	5, 5
月曜日	*getsuyōbi*	Monday	17, 5
火曜日	*kayōbi*	Tuesday	18, 5
水曜日	*suiyōbi*	Wednesday	19, 5

83	几 虫 ｜ 2s/20 64 2	*FŪ, [FU]* – wind; appearance, style **kaze, [kaza]** – wind

風水　*fūsui*　wind and water; feng shui　　　　　　　　　　19
風土　*fūdo*　natural feature, climate　　　　　　　　　　22
日本風　*Nihon-fū*　Japanese-style　　　　　　　　　　5, 23
北風　*kitakaze*　north wind　　　　　　　　　　53

84	田 5f/58	*DEN, ta* – rice field, paddy

水田　*suiden*　rice paddy　　　　　　　　　　19
田中　*Tanaka*　(surname)　　　　　　　　　　26
本田　*Honda*　(surname)　　　　　　　　　　23
山田　*Yamada*　(surname)　　　　　　　　　　31

85	力 十 2f/8 12	**SETSU, [SAI], ki(ru)** – cut **ki(reru)** – cut well; break off; run out of

大切　taisetsu　important; precious　24
一切れ　hitokire　slice, piece　2
切り上げ　kiriage　conclusion; rounding up; revaluation　29
切り下げ　kirisage　reduction; devaluation　28

86	一 亻 丨 0a 3 2	**I-** – (prefix)

以上　ijō　or more; more than; above-mentioned　29
三時間以上　san jikan ijō　at least three hours　4, 34, 35, 29
以下　ika　or less; less than; as follows　28
三つ以下　mittsu ika　three or fewer　4, 28

87	口 3d/24	***KŌ, KU, kuchi*** – mouth; oral; speak; job; beginning	

人口　*jinkō*　population, number of inhabitants　　　　　1
入（り）口　*iriguchi*　entrance　　　　　43
出口　*deguchi*　exit　　　　　44
出入口　*deiriguchi*　entrance/exit　　　　　44, 43

88	目 5c/55	***MOKU, [BOKU], me, [ma]*** – eye, (suffix for ordinals)	

一目　*ichimoku, hitome*　a glance　　　　　2
目上　*meue*　one's superior/senior　　　　　29
目下　*meshita*　one's subordinate/junior　　　　　28
三日目　*mikkame*　on the 3rd day　　　　　4, 5

89	扌 3c/23

SHU, te, [ta] – hand

上手	*jōzu*	skilled, good, good at	29
下手	*heta*	unskilled, poor, poor at	28
手本	*tehon*	model, example, pattern	23
切手	*kitte*	(postage) stamp	85

手　手　手

手　手　手

90	𧾷 7d/70

SOKU – foot, leg; (counter for pairs of footwear) **ashi** – foot, leg **ta(ru), ta(riru)** – be enough, sufficient

一足	*issoku*	1 pair (of shoes/socks)	⌞**ta(su)** – add up, add (to)	2
一足	*hitoashi*	a step		2
手足	*teashi*	hands and feet, limbs		89
足下に	*ashimoto ni*	at one's feet; (watch your) step		28

足　足　足

足　足　足

91	イ 木 一　2a/3　41　1	***TAI, TEI, karada*** – body

人体　*jintai*　the human body　　1
五体　*gotai*　the whole body　　7
大体　*daitai*　gist; on the whole, generally　　24
風体　*fūtai, fūtei*　(outward) appearance　　83

体 体 体

体 体 体

92	目 丨　5c/55　2	***JI, SHI, mizuka(ra)*** – self

自分　*jibun*　oneself, one's own　　32
自体　*jitai*　one's own body; itself　　91
自国　*jikoku*　one's own country　　33
自らの手で　*mizukara no te de*　with one's own hands　　89

自 自 自

自 自 自

93 | 言 | 7a/67

GEN, GON, -koto – word **i(u)** – say

言語	*gengo*	language, speech	48
言明	*genmei*	declaration, definite statement	81
一言	*ichigon, hitokoto*	a word, brief comment	2
小言	*kogoto*	a scolding; complaints, griping	25

言　言　言

言　言　言

94 | 方 | 4h/48

HŌ – direction; side **kata** – person; method; side

一方	*ippō*	one side; on the other hand; only	2
四方	*shihō*	north, south, east, west; all directions	6
八方	*happō*	all directions, all sides	10
方言	*hōgen*	dialect	93

方　方　方

方　方　方

95	牛 犭 4g/47 27	**BUTSU, MOTSU, mono** – object, thing

物

人物	*jinbutsu*	person, personage	1
生物	*seibutsu*	living beings, life	36
見物	*kenbutsu*	sightseeing	46
物語	*monogatari*	tale, story	48

物 物 物

物 物 物

96	一 𠃌 彐 0a 24 39	**JI, [ZU], koto** – thing, affair

事

人事	*jinji*	human/personnel affairs	1
火事	*kaji*	a fire	18
事前／事後	*jizen / jigo*	before/after the fact	38, 39
大事	*daiji*	great thing, important	24

事 事 事

事 事 事

97	一 / 夕 0a/30	**SEKI, yū** – evening	
		一 夕　*isseki*　one evening	2
		夕 方　*yūgata*　evening	94
		夕 日　*yūhi*　evening/setting sun	5
		七 夕　*Tanabata*　Star Festival (July 7)	9

98	一　夕　ト 0a　30　13	**SHI** – death **shi(nu)** – die	
		死 体　*shitai*　dead body, corpse	91
		死 人　*shinin*　dead person, the dead	1
		死 後　*shigo*　after death	39
		水 死　*suishi*　drowning	19

99	辶 月 日 2q/19 43 24	**SHŪ** – week

二週間　*nishūkan*　two weeks　　　　　　　　　　　　3, 35
先週　*senshū*　last week　　　　　　　　　　　　　　41
今週　*konshū*　this week　　　　　　　　　　　　　　42
来週　*raishū*　next week　　　　　　　　　　　　　　50

週

| 週 | 週 | 週 | | | | | | | |

| 週 | 週 | 週 | | | | | | | |

100	一 丆 亅 0a 14 2	**FU, BU** – (prefix) not, un-

不足　*fusoku*　insufficiency, shortage　　　　　　　　90
不十分　*fujūbun*　not enough, inadequate　　　　　12, 32
行方不明　*yukue fumei*　whereabouts unknown, missing　49, 94, 81
不死　*fushi*　immortal　　　　　　　　　　　　　　98

不

| 不 | 不 | 不 | | | | | | | |

| 不 | 不 | 不 | | | | | | | |

101	一 火 艹 0a 44 32	**HATSU, HOTSU** – emit, start from, depart

出発　*shuppatsu*　departure, start out　　44
発明　*hatsumei*　invention　　81
発見　*hakken*　discovery　　46
発行　*hakkō*　publish, issue　　49

102	心 4k/51	**SHIN, kokoro** – heart, mind, core

中心　*chūshin*　center, midpoint　　26
本心　*honshin*　one's real mind; real intention　　23
一心に　*isshin ni*　with singlehearted devotion, fervently　　2

103	田 心 5f/58 51	**SHI, omo(u)** – think, believe

思い出　*omoide*　memories　　　　　　　　　　　　　44
思い出す　*omoidasu*　remember　　　　　　　　　　44
思い切って　*omoikitte*　resolutely, daringly　　　　85
思いやり　*omoiyari*　consideration, sympathy, compassion

思　思　思

思　思　思

104	力 2g/8	**RYOKU, RIKI, chikara** – force, power

体力　*tairyoku*　physical strength　　　　　　　　　91
水力　*suiryoku*　water power, hydraulic power　　　19
風力　*fūryoku*　force of the wind　　　　　　　　　83
人力車　*jinrikisha*　rickshaw　　　　　　　　　　1, 71

力　力　力

力　力　力

105	宀 女 3m/33 25	**AN** – peace, peacefulness **yasu(i)** – cheap

安心　　anshin　　feel relieved/reassured　　102
一安心　hitoanshin　feeling relieved for a while　　2, 102
不安　　fuan　　unease, anxiety, fear　　100
安物　　yasumono　cheap goods, low-quality merchandise　　95

安

安 安 安

安 安 安

106	冂 月 丨 2r 43 2	**YŌ** – business, usage **mochi(iru)** – use

用事　　yōji　　business affair; errand　　96
用語　　yōgo　　(technical) term, vocabulary　　48
男子用　danshiyō　for men, men's　　61, 63
用心　　yōjin　　care, caution　　102

用

用 用 用

用 用 用

107	宀 子 3m/33 6	**JI** – character, letter **aza** – village section	
		国字　*kokuji*　national/Japanese script	33
		ローマ字　*rōmaji*　roman letters	
		字体　*jitai*　form of a character, type font	91
		十字　*jūji*　a cross	12

字

字　字　字

字　字　字

108	亠 乂 2j/11 12	**BUN, MON** – literature, text, sentence **fumi** – letter, note	
		文字　*moji, monji*　letter, character	107
		文学　*bungaku*　literature	65
		本文　*honbun*　text, wording	23
		文明　*bunmei*　civilization	81

文

文　文　文

文　文　文

109 氵 攵 亠
3a/21 25 15

KAI, umi – sea, ocean

大海	taikai	an ocean	24
海外	kaigai	overseas, abroad	58
日本海	Nihonkai	Sea of Japan	5, 23
死海	Shikai	the Dead Sea	98

海　海　海

海　海　海

110 土 十 丨
3b/22 12 2

CHI, JI – earth, land

土地	tochi	land, soil	22
地方	chihō	region, area	94
地名	chimei	place name	57
出生地	shusshōchi, shusseichi	birthplace	44, 36

地　地　地

地　地　地

111	立 5b/54	**RITSU, [RYŪ], ta(tsu)** – stand (up) **ta(teru)** – set up, raise

国立	*kokuritsu*	national, state-supported	33
自立	*jiritsu*	independent, self-supporting	92
中立	*chūritsu*	neutral, neutrality	26
目立つ	*medatsu*	be conspicuous, stick out	88

立　立　立

立　立　立

112	禾 厶 5d/56 17	**SHI, watakushi, watashi** – I; private

私事	*shiji*	personal affairs	96
私物	*shibutsu*	private property	95
私用	*shiyō*	private use	106
私立	*shiritsu*	private, privately supported	111

私　私　私

私　私　私

113	`ヽ ` ` ム` 2o/16 17	**KŌ, ōyake** – public, official

公安　*kōan*　public peace/security　105
公休日　*kōkyūbi*　legal holiday　45, 5
公立　*kōritsu*　public　111
公海　*kōkai*　international waters　109

公

公　公　公

公　公　公

114	`立 日 心` 5b/54 42 51	***I*** – will, heart, mind, thought; meaning, sense

意見　*iken*　opinion　46
用意　*yōi*　preparations, readiness　106
意外　*igai*　unexpected, surprising　58
不意　*fui*　sudden, unexpected　100

意

意　意　意

意　意　意

115	一 二 儿 0a 4 16	**GEN** – origin; (Chinese monetary unit) **GAN** – origin **moto** – origin; (as prefix) former, ex-

元気　*genki*　healthy, peppy　72
元日　*ganjitsu*　New Year's Day　5
元金　*gankin*　principal (vs. interest), principal amount　21
地元　*jimoto*　local　110

元

116	‒/工 0a/38	**KŌ, KU** – artisan, manufacturing, construction

工事　*kōji*　construction　96
大工　*daiku*　carpenter　24
女工　*jokō*　woman factory-worker　62
工学　*kōgaku*　engineering　65

工

117	宀 工 儿 3m/33 38 16	**KŪ, sora** – sky; empty **a(keru), a(ku)** – make unoccupied, be unoccupied **kara** – empty

空気　*kūki*　air — 72
（時間と）空間　*(jikan to) kūkan*　(time and) space — 34, 35, 35
空車　*kūsha*　empty car, For Hire (taxi) — 71
大空　*ōzora*　sky, firmament — 24

空　空　空

空　空　空

118	王 日 土 4f/46 42 22	**RI** – reason, logic, principle

地理（学）　*chiri(gaku)*　geography — 110, 65
心理学　*shinrigaku*　psychology — 102, 65
理事　*riji*　director — 96
理事長　*rijichō*　chairman, president — 96, 60

理　理　理

理　理　理

119	⑴	
	3n/35　2	

SHŌ, suko(shi) – a little, a few **suku(nai)** – little, few

少年	*shōnen*	boy	37
少女	*shōjo*	girl	62
少々	*shōshō*	a little	
少しずつ	*sukoshizutsu*	little by little, a little at a time	

少　少　少

少　少　少

120	⑴		
	2q/19　55　16		

DŌ, [TŌ], michi – road, way, path; dao/tao

国道	*kokudō*	national highway	33
北海道	*Hokkaidō*	Hokkaidō	53, 109
東海道	*Tōkaidō*	the Tōkaidō highway	51, 109
書道	*shodō*	calligraphy	70

道　道　道

道　道　道

121	辶 月 一
	2q/19 43 1

TSŪ, [TSU], tō(ru) – go through, pass **tō(su)** – let through **kayo(u)** – commute

文通	buntsū	correspondence, letter-exchange	108
通学	tsūgaku	attend school	65
大通り	ōdōri	a main street, thoroughfare	24
見通し	mitōshi	prospects, outlook	46

通 通 通

通 通 通

122	土 日 犭
	3b/22 42 27

JŌ, ba – place

工場	kōjō, kōba	factory, plant	116
出場	shutsujō	stage appearance; participation	44
入場	nyūjō	entrance, admission	43
立場	tachiba	standpoint, point of view	111

場 場 場

場 場 場

123	王 丶 4f/46 2	***SHU, [SU]*** – main; master, lord ***nushi*** – owner, master ***omo*** – main, principal

主人　*shujin*　husband, head of household　　　　　　　1
主人公　*shujinkō*　hero, main character　　　　　　1, 113
自主　*jishu*　independence, autonomy　　　　　　　92
地主　*jinushi*　landowner, landlord　　　　　　　110

主　主　主

主　主　主

124	亻 王 丶 2a/3 46 2	***JŪ, su(mu), su(mau)*** – live, dwell, reside

住人　*jūnin*　inhabitant, resident　　　　　　　　1
安住　*anjū*　peaceful living　　　　　　　　　　105
住まい　*sumai*　residence, where one lives, address
住み心地　*sumigokochi*　comfort/coziness (in living), livability　　　102, 110

住　住　住

住　住　住

125	イ 二 ム 2a/3 4 17	**KAI** – meeting, association **E, a(u)** – meet

国会 *kokkai* parliament, Diet, congress　33
大会 *taikai* mass meeting; sports meet, tournament　24
学会 *gakkai* learned/academic society　65
会見 *kaiken* interview, news conference　46

126	⺮ 口 イ 6f/66 24 3	**TŌ, kota(e)** – an answer **kota(eru)** – answer

口答 *kōtō* oral answer　87
名答 *meitō* right/apt/excellent answer　57
口答え *kuchigotae* backtalk, retort　87
手答え *tegotae* response, effect　89

127
門 口
8e/75 24

MON, to(i), [ton] – question, problem **to(u)** – ask, inquire

問答	*mondō*	questions and answers, dialogue	126
自問	*jimon*	question oneself	92
学問	*gakumon*	learning, scholarship, education, science	65
問いただす	*toitadasu*	inquire, question	

128
口 貝
3d/24 68

IN – member

会員	*kaiin*	member (of a society)	125
海員	*kaiin*	seaman, sailor	109
工員	*kōin*	factory worker	116
人員	*jin'in*	staff, personnel	1

129	日 土 丨 4c/42 22 2	**SHA, mono** – person

学者　*gakusha*　scholar　　　　　　　　　　　　　　65
日本学者　*Nihongakusha*　Japanologist　　　　　5, 23, 65
死者　*shisha*　dead person, the dead　　　　　　98
後者　*kōsha*　the latter　　　　　　　　　　　　39

者　者　者

者　者　者

130	宀 犭 乚 3m/33 27 10	**KA, KE, ie, ya** – house, home, family

家事　*kaji*　family affairs; household chores　　　96
国家　*kokka*　state, nation　　　　　　　　　　33
家来　*kerai*　retainer, vassal　　　　　　　　　50
家主　*yanushi*　landlord, house owner　　　　123

家　家　家

家　家　家

131	宀 土 厶 3m/33 22 17	**SHITSU** – a room **muro** – greenhouse, cellar	
		私室 *shishitsu* private room	112
		地下室 *chikashitsu* basement, cellar	110, 28
		分室 *bunshitsu* isolated room; annex	32
		室長 *shitsuchō* senior roommate; section chief	60

室

室 室 室

室 室 室

132	尸 土 厶 3r/40 22 17	**OKU** – house **ya** – roof; house; shop, dealer	
		家屋 *kaoku* house, building	130
		屋上 *okujō* roof, rooftop	29
		小屋 *koya* cottage, hut, shack	25
		八百屋 *yaoya* vegetable shop, greengrocer	10, 14

屋

屋 屋 屋

屋 屋 屋

133	广宀 冂 卜 3q/18 24 13	**TEN, mise** – shop, store

書店　*shoten*　bookstore　　　　　　　　　　　70
本店　*honten*　head office, main shop　　　23
店員　*ten'in*　store employee, clerk　　　128
店先　*misesaki*　storefront　　　　　　　　41

店　店　店

店　店　店

134	十 口 2k/12 24	**KO, furu(i)** – old **furu(su)** – wear out

古風　*kofū*　old customs; antiquated　　　　　　　83
古語　*kogo*　archaic word; old adage　　　　　　48
古今東西　*kokon-tōzai*　all ages and countries　42, 51, 52
古本　*furuhon*　secondhand/used book　　　　　23

古　古　古

古　古　古

135	立 木 斤 5b/54 41 50	**SHIN, atara(shii), ara(ta), nii-** – new

新聞　　*shinbun*　newspaper　　　　　　　　47
古新聞　*furushinbun*　old newspapers　　134, 47
新年　　*shinnen*　the New Year　　　　　　37
新人　　*shinjin*　newcomer, new face　　　　1

新　新　新

新　新　新

136	立 貝 木 5b/54 68 41	**SHIN** – intimacy; parent **oya** – parent **shita(shii)** – intimate, close (friend) **shita(shimu)** – get to

know better　85
親切　*shinsetsu*　kind, friendly
親日　*shin-Nichi*　pro-Japanese　　　　　5
母親　*hahaoya*　mother　　　　　　　　66
親子　*oyako*　parent and child　　　　　63

親　親　親

親　親　親

137	貝 斤
	7b/68 50

SHITSU – quality, nature **SHICHI, [CHI]** – hostage, pawn

質問	*shitsumon*	a question	127
物質	*busshitsu*	matter, material, substance	95
本質	*honshitsu*	essence, substance	23
人質	*hitojichi*	hostage	1

質　質　質

質　質

138	糸 厂 十
	6a/61 18 12

SHI, kami – paper

日本紙	*Nihonshi*	Japanese paper	5, 23
新聞紙	*shinbunshi*	newspaper; newsprint	135, 47
アンケート用紙	*ankēto yōshi*	questionnaire, survey form	106
手紙	*tegami*	letter	89

紙　紙　紙

紙　紙　紙

139 5f/58 14	田 丁	**CHŌ, machi** – town, quarter, street

町人　*chōnin*　merchant; townsfolk　　　　　　　　　1
町会　*chōkai*　town council, town-block association　125
下町　*shitamachi*　(low-lying) downtown area　　　28
室町　*Muromachi*　(historical period, 1392-1573)　131

町　町　町

町　町　町

140 2j/11 24 35	亠 口 小	**KYŌ, KEI** – the capital

東京　*Tōkyō*　Tōkyō　　　　　　　　　　　51
上京　*jōkyō*　go/come to Tōkyō　　　　　29
北京　*Pekin*　Peking, Beijing　　　　　　53
南京　*Nankin*　Nanking　　　　　　　　54

京　京　京

京　京　京

141	冂 卩 一 2r/20 24 1	**DŌ, ona(ji)** – same	
		同時に *dōji ni* at the same time, simultaneously	34
		同年 *dōnen* that (same) year; same age	37
		同意 *dōi* agreement, consent	114
		一同 *ichidō* all concerned, all of us	2

142	⼇ 尸 丨 2n/15 40 2	**SHOKU, SHIKI, iro** – color; erotic passion	
		物色 *busshoku* look for; select	95
		五色 *goshiki* the five colors (red, yellow, blue, black, white); multicolored	7
		色紙 *shikishi* (type of calligraphy paper)	138
		色紙 *irogami* colored paper	138

143	火 日 土 4d/44 42 22	**KOKU, kuro(i), kuro** – black

黒色　*kokushoku*　black　142
黒海　*Kokkai*　the Black Sea　109
黒白　*kuroshiro*　black and/or white; right and wrong　75
黒字　*kuroji*　(in the) black, black figures　107

黒　黒　黒

黒　黒　黒

144	土 儿 3b/22 16	**SEKI, [SHAKU], aka(i), aka** – red **aka(ramu)** – become red, blush **aka(rameru)** – make red, blush

赤十字　*Sekijūji*　Red Cross　12, 107
赤道　*sekidō*　equator　120
赤字　*akaji*　deficit, red figures, (in the) red　107
赤ちゃん　*akachan*　baby

赤　赤　赤

赤　赤　赤

145	月 土 一
	4b/43 22 1

SEI, [SHŌ], ao(i), ao – blue, green; unripe

青年	*seinen*	young man/people	37
青少年	*seishōnen*	young people, youth	119, 37
青空	*aozora*	blue sky	117
青物	*aomono*	green vegetables	95

青

146	日 宀 丨
	4c/42 15 2

TEKI – (attributive suffix); target **mato** – target

的中	*tekichū*	hit the mark, come true, guess right	26
目的	*mokuteki*	purpose, aim, goal	88
一時的	*ichijiteki*	temporary	2, 34
的外れ	*matohazure*	wide of the mark; out of focus	58

的

147	ロ 大 ノ 3d/24 34 15	**CHI, shi(ru)** – know

知

	通知	*tsūchi*	a notification, communication	121
	知事	*chiji*	governor (of a prefecture)	96
	知人	*chijin*	an acquaintance	1
	物知り	*monoshiri*	knowledgeable, erudite; erudite person	95

知　知　知

知　知　知

148	弓 虫 ム 3h/28 64 17	**KYŌ, GŌ, tsuyo(i)** – strong ***tsuyo(maru)*** – become strong(er) ***tsuyo(meru)*** – make strong(er),

強

			strengthen ***shi(iru)*** – force	104
	強力	*kyōryoku*	strength, power	83
	強風	*kyōfū*	strong/high winds	72
	強気	*tsuyoki*	(self-)confidence; bullish (market)	72
	気強い	*kizuyoi*	reassuring; stout-hearted, resolute	72

強　強　強

強　強　強

149	匚 大 ケ 2t/20 34 15	*I* – medicine, healing

医学	*igaku*	medicine	65
医学用語	*igaku yōgo*	medical term	65, 106, 48
医者	*isha*	physician, doctor	129
女医	*joi*	woman physician, lady doctor	62

医

医 医 医

医 医 医

150	方 大 ケ 4h/48 34 15	*ZOKU* – family, tribe

家族	*kazoku*	family	130
親族	*shinzoku*	relative, kin	136
一族	*ichizoku*	one's whole family, kin	2
同族	*dōzoku*	the same family/tribe	141

族

族 族 族

族 族 族

151	方 ケ イ 4h/48 15 3	**RYO, tabi** – trip, travel	

旅行　　*ryokō*　　trip, travel　　　　　　　　　　　　　　　　49
旅行者　*ryokōsha*　traveler, tourist　　　　　　　　　　　49, 129
旅先　　*tabisaki*　 destination　　　　　　　　　　　　　　　41
旅立つ　*tabidatsu*　start on a journey　　　　　　　　　　　111

152	イ 冂 2a/3 20	**NIKU** – meat, flesh; sealing ink	

肉屋　*nikuya*　　butcher (shop)　　　　　　　　　　　　　132
肉体　*nikutai*　　the body, the flesh　　　　　　　　　　　　91
肉親　*nikushin*　 blood relationship/relative　　　　　　　136

153	一 車 一 0a 69 1	**JŪ, CHŌ, omo(i)** – heavy **kasa(naru)** – lie on top of one another **kasa(neru)** – pile on top of one another

体重　taijū　body weight　　　　　　　　　　└**-e** – -fold, -ply　91
重力　jūryoku　gravity, gravitation　　　　　　　　　　　　104
重大　jūdai　weighty, grave, important　　　　　　　　　　24
二重　nijū, futae　double, twofold　　　　　　　　　　　　3

重　重　重

重　重　重

154	一/夕 0a/30	**TA, ō(i)** – much, many, numerous

多少　tashō　much or little, many or few; some　　　　119
多元的　tagenteki　pluralistic　　　　　　　　115, 146
多年生　tanensei　perennial　　　　　　　　　　37, 36

多　多　多

多　多　多

155	口 3d/24	**HIN** – refinement; article **shina** – goods; quality

		上品	jōhin	refined, elegant, graceful	29
		下品	gehin	unrefined, gross, vulgar	28
		品質	hinshitsu	quality	137
		品物	shinamono	merchandise	95

品

品　品　品

品　品　品

156	力 車 丨 2g/8　69　2	**DŌ** – motion **ugo(ku)** – (intr.) move **ugo(kasu)** – (tr.) move

		自動車	jidōsha	automobile, car	92, 71
		動物	dōbutsu	animal	95
		動力	dōryoku	moving force, power	104
		動員	dōin	mobilize	128

動

動　動　動

動　動　動

157 — 一 日 土   0a 42 22

YA, no – field, plain

野生	yasei	wild (animal/plant)	36
野外	yagai	the open air, outdoor	58
分野	bun'ya	field (of endeavor)	32
上野	Ueno	(section of Tōkyō)	29

野 野 野 野

野 野 野

158 — 士 冂 儿   3p/22 20 16

BAI, u(ru) – sell   **u(reru)** – be sold

売店	baiten	stand, newsstand, kiosk	133
売り上げ	uriage	sales	29
売り子	uriko	store salesclerk	63
売り切れ	urikire	sold out	85

売 売 売

売 売 売

159	罒 貝 5g/55 68	**BAI, ka(u)** – buy	

売買　*baibai*　buying and selling, trade, dealing　　158
買い物　*kaimono*　shopping, purchase　　95
買い手　*kaite*　buyer　　89
買い入れる　*kaiireru*　purchase, stock up on　　43

160	攵 土 子 4i/49 22 6	**KYŌ, oshi(eru)** – teach **oso(waru)** – be taught, learn	

教室　*kyōshitsu*　classroom　　131
教員　*kyōin*　teacher, instructor; teaching staff　　128
教会　*kyōkai*　church　　125
教え方　*oshiekata*　teaching method　　94

161	日 十 4c/42 12	**SŌ, [SA'], haya(i)** – early, fast **haya(maru)** – be hasty **haya(meru)** – hasten

早々　*sōsō*　early, immediately
早目に　*hayame ni*　a little early (leaving leeway)　88
早足　*hayaashi*　quick pace, fast walking　90
手早い　*tebayai*　quick, nimble, agile　89

早

早　早　早

早　早　早

162	艹 木 亻 3k/32 41 3	**CHA, SA** – tea

茶色　*chairo*　brown　142
茶室　*chashitsu*　tea-ceremony room　131
茶の間　*cha no ma*　living room　35
茶道　*chadō, sadō*　tea ceremony　120

茶

茶　茶　茶

茶　茶　茶

163	— 卅 一	**SEI, SE, yo** – world, era
	0a 32 1	

二世　*nisei*　second generation　　3
中世　*chūsei*　Middle Ages　　26
世間　*seken*　the world, public, people　　35
出世　*shusse*　success in life, getting ahead　　44

世　世　世

世　世　世

164	卅 亻 ﾄ	**KA, hana** – flower, blossom
	3k/32 3 13	

生け花　*ikebana*　flower arranging　　36
花屋　*hanaya*　flower shop, florist　　132
花見　*hanami*　viewing cherry blossoms　　46
花火　*hanabi*　fireworks　　18

花　花　花

花　花　花

165 亻 戈 2a/3 52	**DAI** – generation; age; price **TAI, ka(waru)** – represent **ka(eru)** – replace **yo** – generation

時代	jidai	era, period			⌐**shiro** – price; substitution	34
古代	kodai	ancient times, antiquity				134
世代	sedai	generation				163
代理	dairi	representation; agent				118

代

代	代	代					

代	代	代					

166 月 十 4b/43 12	**YŪ, U, a(ru)** – be, exist, have

国有	kokuyū	state-owned	33
私有	shiyū	privately-owned	112
有名	yūmei	famous	57
有力	yūryoku	influential, powerful	104

有

有	有	有					

有	有	有					

167	刂 口 宀 2f/16 24 15	***BETSU*** – different, separate, another, special ***waka(reru)*** – diverge, part, bid farewell	
		別人　*betsujin*　different person	1
		別物　*betsumono*　something else, exception, special case	95
		分別　*funbetsu*　discretion, good judgment	32
		別れ目　*wakareme*　turning point, junction, parting of the ways	88

168	⼘ 亠 一 2m 38 1	***SEI, SHŌ, tada(shii)*** – correct, just ***tada(su)*** – correct ***masa (ni)*** – just, exactly, certainly	
		校正　*kōsei*　proofreading	68
		不正　*fusei*　injustice	100
		公正　*kōsei*　fair, just	113
		正月　*shōgatsu*　January; New Year	17

169

一 ヽ 王
0a 16 46

業

GYŌ – occupation, business, undertaking **GŌ** – karma **waza** – act, deed, work, art

工業	kōgyō	industry	116
事業	jigyō	undertaking, enterprise	96
学業	gakugyō	schoolwork, scholastic achievement	65
早業	hayawaza	quick work; sleight of hand	161

業 業 業

業 業 業

170

犭
3g/27

犬

KEN, inu – dog

野犬	yaken	stray dog	157
日本犬	Nihonken	Japanese dog	5, 23
小犬	koinu	puppy	25
犬小屋	inugoya	doghouse	25, 132

犬 犬 犬

犬 犬 犬

171	牛 4g/47

GYŪ, ushi – cow, bull, cattle

牛肉	gyūniku	beef	152
野牛	yagyū	buffalo, bison	157
水牛	suigyū	water buffalo	19
子牛	koushi	calf	63

牛　牛　牛

牛　牛　牛

172	特 4g/47 22 37

TOKU – special

特別	tokubetsu	special	167
特色	tokushoku	distinguishing characteristic	142
特有	tokuyū	characteristic, peculiar (to)	166
特長	tokuchō	strong point, forte	60

特　特　特

特　特　特

| 173 | 馬 尸 乀 |
| 10a/78 40 2 | |

駅

EKI – (train) station

東京駅	*Tōkyō-eki*	Tōkyō Station	51, 140
駅前	*ekimae*	(in) front of/opposite the station	38
駅長	*ekichō*	stationmaster	60
駅員	*ekiin*	station employee	128

駅 駅 駅

駅 駅 駅

| 174 | 鳥 |
| 11b/80 | |

鳥

CHŌ, tori – bird

白鳥	*hakuchō*	swan	75
野鳥	*yachō*	wild bird	157
花鳥	*kachō*	flowers and birds	164
小鳥	*kotori*	(small) bird	25

鳥 鳥 鳥

鳥 鳥 鳥

175	氵 王 儿 3a/21　46　16

YŌ – ocean; foreign, Western

大洋	*taiyō*	ocean	24
東洋	*tōyō*	the East, Orient	51
西洋	*seiyō*	the West, Occident	52
大西洋	*Taiseiyō*	Atlantic Ocean	24, 52

洋　洋　洋

176	魚 11a/79

GYO, sakana, uo – fish

金魚	*kingyo*	goldfish	21
魚肉	*gyoniku*	fish (meat)	152
生魚	*namazakana, seigyo*	raw/fresh fish	36
魚屋	*sakanaya*	fish shop/dealer	132

魚　魚　魚

177	ⁿ 心 ⺕ 2n/15 51 39	**KYŪ** – urgent, sudden **iso(gu)** – be in a hurry

急行	kyūkō	rush, hurry, hasten; express (train, bus, elevator))	49
特急	tokkyū	limited express (train); (at) super speed	172
急用	kyūyō	urgent business	106
大急ぎ	ōisogi	in a big hurry/rush	24

急　急　急

急 急 急

178	心 工 ⼝ 4k/51 38 24	**AKU, O, waru(i)** – bad, evil

悪事	akuji	evil deed	96
悪意	akui	evil intent, malice, ill will	114
悪口	akkō, warukuchi	abusive language, speaking ill of	87
悪者	warumono	bad fellow, scoundrel	129

悪　悪　悪

悪 悪 悪

179	口 木 一
	3d/24 41 1

MI, aji – taste **aji(wau)** – taste, relish, appreciate

意味	imi	meaning, significance, sense	114
正味	shōmi	net (amount/weight/price)	168
不気味	bukimi	uncanny, eerie, ominous	100, 72
地味	jimi	plain, subdued, undemonstrative	110

味　味　味

味　味　味

180	礻 土
	4e/45 22

SHA – Shinto shrine; company; firm **yashiro** – Shinto shrine

社会	shakai	society, social	125
会社	kaisha	company, firm	125
本社	honsha	our company; head office	23
社長	shachō	company president	60

社　社　社

社　社　社

181	銀 食 8a/72 77	**GIN** – silver

銀行　*ginkō*　bank　　　　　　　　　　　　　　　　　49
日銀　*Nichigin*　the Bank of Japan　　　　　　　　　　5
銀色　*gin'iro*　silver color　　　　　　　　　　　　　142
銀メダル　*ginmedaru*　silver medal

銀　銀　銀

銀　銀　銀

182	リ ヨ 巾 2f/16 39 26	**KI, kae(ru)** – return **kae(su)** – let return, dismiss

帰国　*kikoku*　return to one's country　　　　　　　33
帰り道　*kaerimichi*　the way back/home　　　　　　120
日帰り　*higaeri*　go and return in a day　　　　　　　5

帰　帰　帰

帰　帰　帰

183	米 十 丶	**RYŌ** – materials; fee	
	6b/62 12 2		

	料理	*ryōri*	cooking, cuisine; dish, food	118
料	食料	*shokuryō*	food	79
	料金	*ryōkin*	fee, charge, fare	21
	有料	*yūryō*	fee-charging, toll (road), pay (toilet)	166

料　料　料

料　料　料

184	食 夂	**IN, no(mu)** – drink	
	8b/77 49		

	飲食	*inshoku*	food and drink, eating and drinking	79
飲	飲料	*inryō*	drink, beverage	183
	飲み物	*nomimono*	(something to) drink, beverage	95
	飲み水	*nomimizu*	drinking water	19

飲　飲　飲

飲　飲　飲

185	食 厂 又	**HAN, meshi** – cooked rice; meal, food	
	8b/77 18 9	ご飯 *gohan* cooked rice; meal, food	
		赤飯 *sekihan* (festive) rice boiled with red beans	144
		夕飯 *yūhan, yūmeshi* evening meal, supper, dinner	97
		五目飯 *gomokumeshi* a rice, fish, and vegetable dish	7, 88

飯　飯　飯　飯

飯　飯　飯

186	食 宀 尸	**KAN, yakata** – (large) building, hall	
	8b/77 33 40	旅館 *ryokan* Japanese-style inn	151
		水族館 *suizokukan* aquarium	19, 150
		会館 *kaikan* (assembly) hall	125
		本館 *honkan* main building	23

館　館　館　館

館　館　館

187	亻 口 十 2a/3 24 12	**SHI** – use; messenger **tsuka(u)** – use	
		大使　taishi　ambassador	24
		公使　kōshi　minister, envoy	113
		天使　tenshi　angel	73
		使い方　tsukaikata　how to use, way to handle	94

使　使　使

使　使　使

188	亻 士 2a/3 22	**SHI, [JI], tsuka(eru)** – serve	
		仕事　shigoto　work, job	96
		仕立て屋　shitateya　tailor; dressmaker	111, 132
		仕方　shikata　way, method, means	94
		仕上げる　shiageru　finish up, complete	29

仕　仕　仕

仕　仕　仕

189	口 十 丶	**ZU** – drawing, diagram, plan **TO, haka(ru)** – plan	
	3s/24 12 2		

地図　*chizu*　map　　　　　　　　　　　　　110
天気図　*tenkizu*　weather map　　　　　73, 72
意図　*ito*　intention　　　　　　　　　　　114
図書館　*toshokan*　library　　　　　　70, 186

190	言 十	**KEI** – measuring, plan, total **haka(ru)** – measure, compute **haka(rau)** – arrange, dispose of, see about	
	7a/67 12		

時計　*tokei*　clock, watch　　　　　　　　　34
会計　*kaikei*　accounting; paying a bill　　125
生計　*seikei*　livelihood, living　　　　　　36
家計　*kakei*　household finances　　　　　130

191	一 日 丅 0a 42 14	**GA** – picture **KAKU** – stroke (in writing kanji)

画家　*gaka*　painter　130
日本画／洋画　*Nihonga / Yōga*　Japanese-style painting / Western-style painting　5, 23, 175
画用紙　*gayōshi*　drawing paper　106, 138
計画　*keikaku*　plan, project　190

画

192	立 日 5b/54 42	**ON, IN, oto, ne** – sound

発音　*hatsuon*　pronunciation　101
母音　*boin*　vowel　66
足音　*ashioto*　sound of footsteps　90
本音　*honne*　one's true intention　23

音

193	日 大 冂 4c/42 34 20	**El, utsu(su)** – reflect, project **utsu(ru)** – be reflected, projected **ha(eru)** – shine, be brilliant

映画　*eiga*　movie 　　　　　　　　　　　　　　　　　191
映画館　*eigakan*　movie theater 　　　　　　　　　191, 186
上映　*jōei*　showing, screening (of a movie) 　　　　29
夕映え　*yūbae*　the glow of sunset 　　　　　　　　97

194	艹 大 冂 3k/32 34 20	**El** – brilliant, talented, gifted; (short for) England

英気　*eiki*　energetic spirit, enthusiasm 　　　　　　72
英語　*Eigo*　the English language 　　　　　　　　　48
英会話　*Ei-kaiwa*　English conversation 　　　　125, 76
日英　*Nichi-Ei*　Japan and Britain/England 　　　　　5

195

頁 日 一
9a/76 42 14

題

1 2 10
3 11
4
12 13
5
6 7 17 18
8
9

DAI – topic, theme, title

問題　*mondai*　problem, question, issue　127
出題　*shutsudai*　propose a question, set a problem　44
話題　*wadai*　topic　76
題名　*daimei*　title　57

題 題 題

題 題 題

196

氵 王 丶
3a/21 46 2

注

1 4
2 5 6
7
8
3

CHŪ – note, comment **soso(gu)** – pour, flow

注意　*chūi*　attention, caution, warning　114
注目　*chūmoku*　attention, notice　88
注文　*chūmon*　order, commission　108
発注　*hatchū*　ordering　101

注 注 注

注 注 注

| 197 | 木 日 ⁊ | **GAKU** – music **RAKU** – pleasure **tano(shimu)** – enjoy **tano(shii)** – fun, enjoyable, pleasant |
| | 4a/41 42 5 | |

音楽　*ongaku*　music　192
文楽　*bunraku*　Japanese puppet theater　108
楽天家　*rakutenka*　optimist　73, 130
安楽死　*anrakushi*　euthanasia　105, 98

楽

| 198 | 亻 宀 ト | **SAKU, SA, tsuku(ru)** – make |
| | 2a/3 15 13 | |

作家　*sakka*　writer　130
作品　*sakuhin*　literary work　155
作り話　*tsukuribanashi*　made-up story, fabrication　76
手作り　*tezukuri*　handmade　89

作

199	土 弓 ト 3b/22 28 13	**KI** – awakening, rise, beginning **o(kiru)** – get/wake/be up **o(koru)** – occur **o(kosu)** – give rise to;

起業   *kigyō*   start a business, organize an undertaking   ⌐wake (someone) up   169
発起人   *hokkinin*   promoter, originator   101, 1
早起き   *hayaoki*   get up early   161
起き上がる *okiagaru* get up, pick oneself up   29

起 *起* *起*

起 *起* *起*

200	广 艹 又 3q/18 32 9	**DO, [TAKU], [TO]** – degree, measure, limit; times **tabi** – times

一度   *ichido*   once; 1 degree (temperature; angle)   2
今度   *kondo*   this time; soon; next time   42
年度   *nendo*   business/fiscal year   37
度重なる *tabikasanaru* repeatedly   153

度 *度* *度*

度 *度* *度*

201	疒 一 冂 5i/60 14 20	**BYŌ, [HEI], ya(mu)** – fall ill, suffer from **yamai** – illness	

病気　byōki　sickness, disease　　　　　　　　　　72
重病　jūbyō　serious illness　　　　　　　　　　　153
急病　kyūbyō　sudden illness　　　　　　　　　　177
病人　byōnin　sick person　　　　　　　　　　　　1

病　病　病

病　病　病

202	欠 口 丁 4j/49 24 14	**KA, uta** – poem, song **uta(u)** – sing	

歌手　kashu　singer　　　　　　　　　　　　　　89
歌人　kajin　poet　　　　　　　　　　　　　　　1
国歌　kokka　national anthem　　　　　　　　　33
校歌　kōka　school song　　　　　　　　　　　　68

歌　歌　歌

歌　歌　歌

203	門 艹 一 8e/75 32 1	**KAI** – opening, development **a(ku)** – (intr.) open **a(keru)** – (tr.) open **hira(keru)** – become developed

公開　　kōkai　　open to the public ⌊**hira(ku)** – (tr. or intr.) open　113
開会　　kaikai　　opening of a meeting　　　　　　　　　　　　　　　125
開発　　kaihatsu　development　　　　　　　　　　　　　　　　　　101

204	゛ 弓 ｜ 2o/16 28 2	**TEI, [DAI], [DE], otōto** – younger brother

子弟　　shitei　　sons, children　　　　　　　　　　　　　　　　　　63
弟子　　deshi　　pupil, apprentice, disciple　　　　　　　　　　　　63
弟子入り　deshiiri　becoming a pupil, entering an apprenticeship　63, 43
弟分　　otōtobun　like a younger brother　　　　　　　　　　　　　32

205 冂 儿 3d/24 16

KEI, [KYŌ], ani – elder brother

兄弟	*kyōdai*	brothers; brothers and sisters	204
父兄	*fukei*	parents and brothers; guardians	67
長兄	*chōkei*	eldest brother	60
兄さん	*niisan*	elder brother	

兄 兄 兄

兄 兄 兄

206 女 巾 宀 3e/25 26 11

SHI, ane – elder sister

長姉	*chōshi*	eldest sister	29
姉上	*aneue*	elder sister (humble)	60
姉さん	*nēsan*	elder sister; young lady	

姉 姉 姉

姉 姉 姉

207	女 木 一 3e/25 41 1	**MAI, imōto** – younger sister

姉妹　*shimai*　sisters　　　　　　　　　　　206
弟妹　*teimai*　younger brothers and sisters　204

208	土 厶 3b/22 17	**KYO, KO, sa(ru)** – leave, move away; pass, elapse

去年　*kyonen*　last year　　　　　　　　　　37
死去　*shikyo*　death　　　　　　　　　　　98
去来　*kyorai*　coming and going　　　　　50
立ち去る　*tachisaru*　leave, go away　　111

209	十 冒 儿 2k/12 55 16	**SHIN** – truth, genuineness, reality **ma** – true, pure, exactly

真理　*shinri*　truth　　　　　　　　　　　　　　118
真空　*shinkū*　vacuum　　　　　　　　　　　　117
真南　*maminami*　due south　　　　　　　　　　54
真ん中　*mannaka*　serious-minded, earnest, honest　26

210	土 ト イ 3b/22 13 3	**SŌ, hashi(ru)** – run

走行　*sōkō*　travel, cover distance　　　　　　　49
走り書き　*hashirigaki*　flowing/hasty handwriting　70
先走る　*sakibashiru*　be forward/impertinent　　41
口走る　*kuchibashiru*　babble, blurt out　　　　87

211	3n/35 13 11	**HO, BU, [FU], aru(ku), ayu(mu)** – walk

歩道　*hodō*　footpath　120
歩行者　*hokōsha*　pedestrian　49, 129
一歩　*ippo*　a step　2
日歩　*hibu*　interest per 100 yen per day　5

212	7c/69 4 17	**TEN, koro(bu), koro(garu), koro(geru)** – roll over, fall down **koro(gasu)** – roll, knock down

自転車　*jitensha*　bicycle　92, 71
転出　*tenshutsu*　move out, be transferred　44
空転　*kūten*　idling (of an engine); getting nowhere　117
七転び八起き　*nanakorobi yaoki*　ups and downs of life　9, 10, 199

213 集

隹 木
8c/73 41

SHŪ, atsu(maru), tsudo(u) – (intr.) gather **atsu(meru)** – (tr.) gather

集金	shūkin	bill collecting	21
集中	shūchū	concentrating	26
特集	tokushū	special edition	172
人集め	hitoatsume	assembling/gathering people together	1

214 運

辶 車 冂
2q/19 69 20

UN – fate, luck **hako(bu)** – carry, transport

運転手	untenshu	driver, chauffeur	212, 89
運動	undō	motion; exercise; a movement	156
運動不足	undō-busoku	lack of exercise	156, 100, 90
不運	fuun	misfortune	100

215	辶 大 儿 2q/19 34 16	**SŌ, oku(ru)** – send

運送　*unsō*　transport, shipment　214
送金　*sōkin*　remittance　21
送別会　*sōbetsukai*　going-away/farewell party　167, 125
見送る　*miokuru*　see (someone) off; escort　46

送 送 送

送 送 送

216	辶 斤 2q/19 50	**KIN, chika(i)** – near, close

中近東　*Chūkintō*　the Near and Middle East　26, 51
近代　*kindai*　modern times, modern　165
近道　*chikamichi*　shortcut, shorter way　120
近づく　*chikazuku*　come/go near, approach

近 近 近

近 近 近

217	扌 土 寸	***JI, mo(tsu)*** – have, possess, hold, maintain	
	3c/23 22 37	持ち主 *mochinushi* owner, possessor	123
		金持ち *kanemochi* rich person	21
		気持ち *kimochi* mood, feeling	72
		長持ち *nagamochi* be durable, last	60

持

持 持 持

持 持 持

218	彳 土 寸	***TAI, ma(tsu)*** – wait for	
	3i/29 22 37	特待 *tokutai* special treatment, distinction	172
		待ち時間 *machi jikan* waiting (time), queuing time	34, 35
		待ちぼうけ *machibōke* getting stood up	
		心待ち *kokoromachi* expectation, anticipation	102

待

待 待 待

待 待 待

219	田 亻 儿 5f/58 3 16	***KAI*** – world; boundary

界

世界	*sekai*	world	163
学界	*gakkai*	academic world	65
外界	*gaikai*	external world, outside	58
下界	*gekai*	this world, the earth below	28

界 界 界

界 界 界

220	糸 夂 丶 6a/61 49 2	***SHŪ, o(waru)*** – come to an end ***o(eru)*** – bring to an end

終

終日	*shūjitsu*	all day long	5
終業	*shūgyō*	close of work/school	169
終電	*shūden*	the last train/streetcar for the day	64

終 終 終

終 終 終

221   夂 丶   4i/49   2

TŌ, fuyu – winter

立冬	*rittō*	first day of winter	111
真冬	*mafuyu*	midwinter, dead of winter	209
冬物	*fuyumono*	winter clothing	95
冬空	*fuyuzora*	winter sky	117

冬 冬 冬

冬 冬 冬

222   日 大 二   4c/42   34   4

SHUN, haru – spring

春分（の日）	*shunbun (no hi)*	vernal equinox	32, 5
立春	*risshun*	beginning of spring	111
青春	*seishun*	springtime of life, youth	145
売春	*baishun*	prostitution	158

春 春 春

春 春 春

223	夊 目 一 4i/49 55 14	**KA, [GE], natsu** – summer	
		立夏　*rikka*　beginning of summer	111
		真夏　*manatsu*　midsummer, height of summer	209
		夏物　*natsumono*　summer clothing	95
		夏休み　*natsuyasumi*　summer vacation	45

夏　夏　夏

夏　夏　夏

224	禾 火 5d/56 44	**SHŪ, aki** – fall, autumn	
		春夏秋冬　*shunkashūtō*　all the year round	222, 223, 221
		春秋　*shunjū*　spring and autumn; years, age	222
		秋分（の日）　*shūbun (no hi)*　autumnal equinox	32, 5
		秋風　*akikaze*　autumn breeze	83

秋　秋　秋

秋　秋　秋

225	月 日 十 4b/43 42 12	**CHŌ** – morning; dynasty **asa** – morning

朝食　chōshoku　breakfast 79
朝日　asahi　morning/rising sun 5
毎朝　maiasa　every morning 69
今朝　kesa, konchō　this morning 42

朝　朝　朝

朝　朝　朝

226	日 尸 一 4c/42 40 1	**CHŪ, hiru** – daytime, noon

昼食　chūshoku　lunch 79
白昼に　hakuchū ni　in broad daylight 75
昼飯　hirumeshi　lunch 185
昼休み　hiruyasumi　lunch break, noon recess 45

昼　昼　昼

昼　昼　昼

227	一 夕 亻 2j/11　30　3	**YA, yoru, yo** – night

夜　　chūya　　day and night　　　　　　　　　　　　　　　　226
今夜　　kon'ya　　tonight　　　　　　　　　　　　　　　　　　42
夜行　　yakō　　traveling by night; night train　　　　　　　49
夜明け　　yoake　　dawn, daybreak　　　　　　　　　　　　81

228	止 卜 2m/13　11	**SHI, to(maru)** – come to a stop **to(meru)** – bring to a stop

終止　　shūshi　　termination　　　　　　　　　　　　　　　220
中止　　chyūshi　　discontinue, suspend, cancel　　　　　　26
通行止め　　tsūkōdome　　Road Closed, No Thoroughfare　　121, 49
口止め料　　kuchidomeryō　　hush money　　　　　　　　87, 183

229 口 厶
3d/24 17

DAI, TAI – stand, pedestal; platform, plateau

天文台	*tenmondai*	observatory	73, 108
高台	*takadai*	high ground, a height	74
台本	*daihon*	script, screenplay, libretto	23
台風	*taifū*	typhoon	83

台	台	台						
台	台	台						

230 女 口 厶
3e/25 24 17

SHI, haji(maru) – (intr.) start, begin **haji(meru)** – (tr.) start, begin

開始	*kaishi*	beginning, opening	203
始終	*shijū*	from first to last, all the while	220
始業	*shigyō*	begin work, open	169
年始	*nenshi*	beginning of the year, New Year's	37

始	始	始						
始	始	始						

231	⺌ 口 土 3n/35 24 22

堂

DŌ – temple; hall

食堂	*shokudō*	dining hall, restaurant	79
公会堂	*kōkaidō*	public hall, community center	113, 125
本堂	*hondō*	main temple building	23
堂々と	*dōdō to*	majestic, grand, magnificent	

堂 堂 堂

堂 堂 堂

232	言 戈 工 7a/67 52 38

試

SHI, kokoro(miru), tame(su) – give it a try, try out, attempt

試作	*shisaku*	trial manufacture/cultivation	198
試食	*shishoku*	sample, taste	79
試運転	*shiunten*	trial run	214, 212
入試	*nyūshi*	touchstone, test	43

試 試 試

試 試 試

233	馬 口 亻
	10a/78 24 3

KEN – effect; testing **[GEN]** – beneficial effect

試験	shiken	examination, test	232
入学試験	nyūgaku shiken	entrance exam	43, 65, 232
体験	taiken	experience	91
先験的	senkenteki	transcendental, a priori	41, 146

驗 驗 驗

驗 驗 驗

234	冖 十 一
	2i/20 12 1

SHA, utsu(su) – copy down, copy, duplicate; depict; photograph **utsu(ru)** – be taken, turn out (photo)

写真	shashin	photograph	209
写本	shahon	manuscript, handwritten copy, codex	23
写生	shasei	sketch, painting from nature	36
生き写し	ikiutsushi	close resemblance	36

写 写 写

写 写 写

235	十 土 一 2k 22 1	***KŌ, kanga(eru)*** – think, consider

考

一考	*ikkō*	consideration, a thought	2
思考	*shikō*	thinking, thought	103
考古学	*kōkogaku*	archaeology	134, 65
考え方	*kangaekata*	way of thinking, viewpoint	94

考 考 考

考 考 考

236	氵 艹 日 3a/21 32 24	***KAN*** – Han (Chinese dynasty); China; man, fellow

漢

漢字	*kanji*	kanji, Chinese character	107
漢文	*kanbun*	Chinese writing; Chinese classics	108
漢方	*kanpō*	Chinese herbal medicine	94
悪漢	*akkan*	scoundrel, villain	178

漢 漢 漢

漢 漢 漢

237

習

羽 ヨ 丨
4c/42　39　2

SHŪ, nara(u) – learn

学習	gakushū	learning, study	65
自習	jishū	studying by oneself	92
習字	shūji	penmanship, calligraphy	107
手習い	tenarai	practice penmanship; learning	89

習　習　習

習　習　習

238

院

阝 宀 二
2d/7　33　4

IN – institution; house (of a legislature), parliament

病院	byōin	hospital	201
入院	nyūin	admission to a hospital	43
大学院	daigakuin	graduate school	24, 65
院長	inchō	head of the hospital/school/institute	60

院　院　院

院　院　院

239	ⸯ 耳 王 2o/16 55 46

CHAKU, [JAKU] – arrival; clothing **ki(ru), tsu(keru)** – put on, wear **ki(seru)** – dress (someone)

一着	itchaku	first arrival; first (in a race); a suit (of clothes)	⌊**tsu(ku)** – arrive	2
着手	chakushu	start, commence, proceed with		89
着物	kimono	kimono; clothing		95
下着	shitagi	underwear		28

着

着 着 着

着 着 着

240	月 阝 又 4b/43 7 9

FUKU – clothes, dress; obey, serve; dose

夏服	natsufuku	summer clothes/wear	223
洋服	yōfuku	Western clothing	175
心服	shinpuku	admiration and devotion	102
着服	chakufuku	embezzlement, misappropriation	239

服

服 服 服

服 服 服

| 241 | 广 ム 3q/18 17 | **KŌ, hiro(i)** – broad, wide **hiro(geru)** – extend, enlarge **hiro(garu)** – spread, expand **hiro(meru)** – broaden, propagate **hiro(maru)** – spread, be propagated |

広大	*kōdai*	vast, extensive, huge	24
公言	*kōgen*	bragging, boastful speech	113, 93
広場	*hiroba*	plaza, public square	122

広 広 広

広 広 広

| 242 | ク 口 儿 2n/15 24 16 | **BEN** – effort, hard work |

勉強	*benkyō*	studying; diligence; sell cheap	148
勉強家	*benkyōka*	diligent student; hard worker	148, 130
勉学	*bengaku*	study, pursuit of one's studies	65
不勉強	*fubenkyō*	idleness, failure to study	100, 148

勉 勉 勉

勉 勉 勉

243	貝 戈 イ 7b/68 52 3

TAI, ka(su) – rent out, lend

貸し家　*kashiya*　house for rent, rented house　　130
貸しボート　*kashibōto*　boat for rent, rented boat
貸し出す　*kashidasu*　lend/hire out　　44
貸し切り　*kashikiri*　reservations, booking　　85

貸　貸　貸　貸

貸　貸　貸

244	イ 日 艹 2a/3 42 32

SHAKU, ka(riru) – borrow, rent

借金　*shakkin*　debt　　21
貸借　*taishaku*　debits and credits　　243
借用　*shakuyō*　borrowing, loan　　106
転借　*tenshaku*　subleasing　　212

借　借　借　借

借　借　借

245	辶 ヨ 十
	2q/19 39 12

KEN, [KON], ta(teru) – build **ta(tsu)** – be built

建国	kenkoku	founding of a country	33
建立	konryū	erection, building	111
建物	tatemono	a building	95
建て前	tatemae	erection of the framework; principle	38

建

建 建 建

建 建 建

246	宀 儿 十
	3m/33 16 12

KYŪ, kiwa(meru) – investigate thoroughly/exhaustively

究明	kyūmei	study, investigation, inquiry	81
考究	kōkyū	investigation, inquiry, research	235
学究	gakkyū	scholar, student	65

究

究 究 究

究 究 究

247	石 ⼗ 一
	5a/53 32 1

KEN, to(gu) – whet, hone, sharpen; polish, wash (rice)

研究	kenkyū	research	246
研究室	kenkyūshitsu	laboratory, study room	246, 131
研究家	kenkyūka	researcher, student of	246, 130
研学	kengaku	study	65

研 研 研

研 研 研

248 耳 6e/65

JI, mimi – ear

耳目	*jimoku*	eye and ear; attention, notice	88
中耳	*chūji*	the middle ear	26
耳たぶ	*mimitabu*	earlobe	
早耳	*hayamimi*	quick-eared, in the know	161

249 一 月 丨 0a 43 2

SHIN, mi – body; one's person

身体	*shintai*	the body	91
出身	*...shusshin*	(be) from ...	44
前身	*zenshin*	one's past life; predecessor	38
身分	*mibun*	one's social standing; identity	32

250 耳 又 6e/65 9

SHU, to(ru) – take

取り出す	*toridasu*	take out; pick out	44
足取り	*ashidori*	way of walking, gait	90
聞き取る	*kikitoru*	catch, follow (what someone says)	47
日取り	*hidori*	appointed day	5

251 ⺌ 彐 3n/35 39

TŌ, a(teru), a(taru) – hit, be on target

本当	*hontō*	truth; really	23
当時	*tōji*	at present; at that time	34
当分	*tōbun*	for now, for a while	32
一人当たり	*hitoriatari*	per person, per capita	2, 1

252	石 5a/53	**SEKI, [SHAKU], ishi** – stone **[KOKU]** – (unit of volume, about 180 liters)		
		石けん　sekken　soap		
		木石　bokuseki　trees and stones; inanimate objects		20
		小石　koishi　small stone, pebble		25
		石切り　ishikiri　stonecutting, quarrying		85

253	一　亻　冂 0a／3　20	**NAI, [DAI], uchi** – inside		
		国内　kokunai　domestic, internal		33
		内外　naigai　inner and outer; domestic and foreign		58
		家内　kanai　my wife; family, home		130
		年内に　nennai ni　before the year is out		37

254	阝　立　口 2d／7　54　24	**BU** – part, section; copy of a publication		
		一部　ichibu　a part; a copy (of a publication)		2
		部分　bubun　a part		32
		本部　honbu　headquarters		23
		部屋　heya　room, apartment		132

255	亻　王 2a／3　46	**ZEN, matta(ku)** – all, whole, entirely **sube(te)** – all		
		全部　zenbu　all		254
		全国　zenkoku　the whole country		33
		全体　zentai　the whole, (in) all		91
		全身　zenshin　the entire body		249

256
口
3s/24

KAI, [E] – times, repetitions **mawa(su)** – send around, rotate **mawa(ru)** – go around, revolve

十回	*jikkai, jukkai* 10 times	12
今回／前回	*konkai / zenkai* this time / last time	42, 38
言い回し	*iimawashi* expression, turn of phrase	93
上回る	*uwamawaru* be more than, exceed	29

257
心 土 宀
4k/51 22 15

SEI – sex; nature (of) **SHŌ** – temperament, propensity

中性	*chūsei* neuter (gender); neutrality (in chemistry)	26
女性	*josei* woman; feminine gender	62
男性	*dansei* man, male; masculinity	61
性分	*shōbun* nature, temperament	32

258
女 子
3e/25 6

KŌ, kono(mu), su(ku) – like

好物	*kōbutsu* favorite food	95
好人物	*kōjinbutsu* good-natured person	1, 95
物好き	*monozuki* idle curiosity	95
大好き	*daisuki* like very much	24

259
亠 儿 十
2j/11 16 12

KŌ – intersection; coming and going **ma(jiru), ma(zaru)** – (intr.) mix **maji(eru), ma(zeru)** – (tr.) mix **maji(waru), ka(u)** – associate (with) **ka(wasu)** – exchange (greetings)

国交	*kokkō* diplomatic relations	33
外交	*gaikō* foreign policy, diplomacy	58
交通	*kōtsū* traffic, transport, communication	121

260	亻 十 丨 2a/3 12 2	**TA, hoka** – other, another	
他		他人　*tanin*　another person; stranger	1
		他国　*takoku*　another/foreign country	33
		他方　*tahō*　the other side/party/direction	94
		自他　*jita*　oneself and others	92

他　他　他

他　他　他

261	亻 立 2a/3 54	**I, kurai** – rank, position	
位		地位　*chii*　position, rank	110
		学位　*gakui*　academic degree	65
		上位　*jōi*　higher rank	29
		位取り　*kuraidori*　position (before/after decimal point)	250

位　位　位

位　位　位

262	氵 土 厶 3a/21 22 17	**HŌ, HA', HO'** – law	
法		国法　*kokuhō*　laws of the country	33
		文法　*bunpō*　grammar	108
		方法　*hōhō*　method	94
		法度　*hatto*　law; prohibition, ban	200

法　法　法

法　法　法

263	禾 口 5d/56 24	**WA, [O]** – peace, harmony; (short for) Japanese *yawa(rageru), yawa(ragu), nago(mu)* – soften, calm	
和			down *nago(yaka)* – mild, gentle, congenial
		和文　*wabun*　Japanese script	108
		和風　*wafū*　Japanese style	83
		不和　*fuwa*　disharmony, discord, enmity	100
		大和　*Yamato*　(old) Japan	24

和　和　和

和　和　和

264
厂 日 小
2p/18 42 35

GEN – original, fundamental *hara* – plain, field, wilderness

原文	*genbun*	the text, the original	108
原子	*genshi*	atom	63
原子力	*genshiryoku*	atomic energy, nuclear power	63, 104
野原	*nohara*	field, plain	157

265
ツ 儿 一
3n/35 16 1

KŌ, hikari – light *hika(ru)* – shine

日光	*nikkō*	sunlight, sunshine	5
月光	*gekkō*	moonlight	17
光年	*kōnen*	light-year	37
発光	*hakkō*	luminosity, emit light	101

266
木 目
4a/41 55

SŌ – aspect, phase **SHŌ** – (government) minister *ai-* – together, fellow, each other

相当	*sōtō*	suitable, appropriate	251
法相	*hōshō*	Minister of Justice	262
外相	*gaishō*	foreign minister	58
相手	*aite*	the other party, partner, opponent	89

267
心 目 木
4k/51 55 41

SŌ, [SO] – idea, thought

思想	*shisō*	idea, thought	103
回想	*kaisō*	retrospection, reminiscense	256
理想	*risō*	an ideal	118
空想	*kūsō*	fantasy, daydream	117

268	2o/16 55 14

SHU, kubi – neck, head

首相	shushō	prime minister	266
部首	bushu	radical of a kanji	254
百人一首	Hyakunin isshu	100 poems by 100 poets (anthology from 1235)	14, 1, 2
手首	tekubi	wrist	89

269	7d/70 49 24

RO, -ji – street, way

道路	dōro	street, road	120
路上	rojō	on the road	29
十字路	jūjiro	intersection, crossroads	12, 107
家路	ieji	one's way home	130

270	4m/40 50

SHO, tokoro – place

住所	jūsho	address; residence, domicile	124
名所	meisho	noted place, sights (to see)	57
所長	shochō	director, head manager	60
長所	chōsho	strong point, merit, advantage	60

271	2a/3 67

SHIN – faith, trust, belief

信用	shin'yō	trust	106
不信	fushin	bad faith, insincerity; distrust	100
自信	jishin	(self-)confidence	92
通信	tsūshin	communication, correspondence, dispatch	121

272

イ ロ 一
2a/3 24 1

GŌ, GA', [KA'], a(u) – fit **a(waseru), a(wasu)** – put together

合意	*gōi* mutual consent, agreement	114
場合	*baai, bawai* (in this) case	122
(お)見合い	*(o)miai* marriage interview	46
間に合う	*maniau* be in time (for); will do, suffice	35

273

⺌ 火 ロ
2m/13 44 24

TEN – point

出発点	*shuppatsuten* starting point	44, 101
原点	*genten* starting point; origin (of coordinate)	264
合点	*gaten, gatten* understanding; consent	272
点字	*tenji* Braille	107

274

尸 ロ 一
3r/40 24 1

KYOKU – bureau, office

当局	*tōkyoku* the authorities, responsible officials	251
局長	*kyokuchō* director of a bureau; postmaster	60
局員	*kyokuin* staff member of a bureau	128
局外者	*kyokugaisha* outsider, onlooker	58, 129

275

尸 ロ 十
3r/40 24 12

KYO, i(ru) – be (present), exist

住居	*jūkyo* dwelling, residence	124
居住地	*kyojūchi* place of residence	124, 110
居間	*ima* living room	35
長居	*nagai* stay (too) long	60

276

| 0a | 40 | 12 |

MIN, tami – people, nation

国民	kokumin	people, nation, citizen	33
人民	jinmin	the people, citizens	1
民主的	minshuteki	democratic	123, 146
民間	minkan	private (not public)	35

民　民　民

民　民　民

277

| 3m/33 | 12 | 2 |

TAKU – house, home, residence

住宅	jūtaku	house, residence	124
自宅	jitaku	one's own home, private residence	92
私宅	shitaku	one's private residence	112
宅地	takuchi	land for housing, residential site	110

宅　宅　宅

宅　宅　宅

278

| 3m/33 | 42 | 3 |

SHUKU, yado – lodging, inn **yado(ru)** – take shelter; be pregnant **yado(su)** – give shelter,

下宿	geshuku	room and board; boardinghouse	⌐conceive (a child) 28
合宿	gasshuku	lodging together	272
民宿	minshuku	tourist home, bed-and-breakfast	276
宿屋	yadoya	inn	132

宿　宿　宿

宿　宿　宿

279

| 2j/11 | 26 |

SHI – city, town, market **ichi** – market

市長	shichō	mayor	60
市民	shimin	citizen, townspeople	276
市立	shiritsu	municipal	111
市場	ichiba, shijō	marketplace, market	122

市　市　市

市　市　市

280

番

5f/58 62 2

BAN – keeping watch; number; order

一番	*ichiban*	the first; number one, most	2
二番目	*nibanme*	the second, number 2	3, 88
番地	*banchi*	lot/house number	110
交番	*kōban*	police box	259

281

術

3i/29 41 4

JUTSU – art, technique, means, conjury

手術	*shujutsu*	(surgical) operation	89
手術室	*shujutsushitsu*	operating room	89, 131
学術	*gakujutsu*	science, learning	65
学術用語	*gakujutsu yōgo*	technical term	65, 106, 48

282

都

2d/7 42 22

TO, TSU, miyako – capital (city)

(大)都市	*(dai)toshi*	(major/large) city	24, 279
都会	*tokai*	city	125
首都	*shuto*	capital (city)	268
都合	*tsugō*	circumstances, reasons	272

283

付

2a/3 37

FU, tsu(ku) – be attached, belong (to) **tsu(keru)** – attach, apply

交付	*kōfu*	deliver, hand over	259
日付け	*hizuke*	date (of a letter)	5
気付く	*kizuku*	(take) notice	72
付き物	*tsukimono*	what (something) entails, adjunct	95

284	艹 儿 一 3k/32 16 1	**KYŌ** – together; (short for) communism **tomo** – together **-tomo** – including

共学　kyōgaku　coeducation　65
共通　kyōtsū　(in) common (with)　121
公共　kōkyō　the public, community　113
共和国　kyōwakoku　republic　263, 33

共 共 共

共 共 共

285	亻 艹 儿 2a/3 32 16	**KYŌ, [KU]** – offer **sona(eru)** – make an offering, dedicate **tomo** – attendant, companion

供出　kyōshutsu　delivery　44
自供　jikyō　confession, admission　92
供物　kumotsu　votive offering　95
子供　kodomo　child　63

供 供 供

供 供 供

286	口 冂 丨 3d/24 20 2	**KŌ, mu(kau)** – face (toward), proceed (to) **mu(keru)** – (tr.) turn **mu(ku)** – (intr.) turn

方向　hōkō　direction　⌐mu(kō) – opposite side　94
向上　kōjō　elevation, betterment　29
意向　ikō　intention, inclination　114
外人向け　gaijinmuke　for foreigners　58, 1

向 向 向

向 向 向

287	一 ⺊ 冂 0a 36 20	**RYŌ** – both, (obsolete Japanese coin)

両親　ryōshin　parents　136
両方　ryōhō　both　94
両手　ryōte　both hands　89
車両　sharyō　car, vehicle　71

両 両 両

両 両 両

288 満

氵 艹 屮
3a/21 32 36

MAN – full; (short for) Manchuria **mi(chiru)** – become full **mi(tasu)** – fill, fulfill

満足	*manzoku*	satisfaction	90
不満	*fuman*	dissatisfaction, discontent	100
満員	*man'in*	full to capacity	128
満点	*manten*	perfect score	273

289 平

十 丆 儿
2k 14 16

HEI, BYŌ, tai(ra), hira – flat, level

平行	*heikō*	parallel	49
平和	*heiwa*	peace	263
不平	*fuhei*	discontent, complaint	100
平方メートル	*heihōmētoru*	square meter	94

290 実

宀 大 二
3m/33 34 4

JITSU – truth, actuality **mi** – fruit, nut **mino(ru)** – bear fruit

事実	*jijitsu*	fact	96
口実	*kōjitsu*	pretext, excuse	87
実行	*jikkō*	put into practice, carry out, realize	49
実力	*jitsuryoku*	actual ability, competence	104

291 情

忄 月 龶
4k/51 43 22

JŌ, [SEI], nasa(ke) – emotion, sympathy

人情	*ninjō*	human feelings, humanity	1
同情	*dōjō*	sympathy	141
事情	*jijō*	circumstances, situation	96
実情	*jitsujō*	actual situation, the facts	290

292

糸 ⼓ ⼂
6a/61　15　2

YAKU – approximately; promise

公約	*kōyaku*	public commitment	113
口約	*kōyaku*	verbal promise	87
約三キロ	*yaku san kiro*	approximately 3 km/kg	4
先約	*sen'yaku*	previous engagement	41

約　約　約

約　約　約

293

弓 ｜
3h/28　2

IN, hi(ku) – pull, attract **hi(keru)** – be ended; make cheaper

引力	*inryoku*	attraction, gravitation	104
引用	*in'yō*	quotation, citation	106
引き出し	*hikidashi*	drawer	44
取り引き	*torihiki*	transaction, trade	250

引　引　引

引　引　引

294

米
6b/62

BEI – rice; (short for) America **MAI, kome** – rice

米食	*beishoku*	rice diet	79
日米	*Nichi-Bei*	Japan and America, Japanese-U.S.	5
白米	*hakumai*	polished rice	75
新米	*shinmai*	new rice; novice	135

米　米　米

米　米　米

295

夂 米 女
4i/49　62　25

SŪ, [SU], kazu – number **kazo(eru)** – count

数字	*sūji*	digit, numeral, figures	107
数学	*sūgaku*	mathematics	65
人数	*ninzū*	number of people	1
手数	*tesū*	trouble, bother	89

数　数　数

数　数　数

296 頁 米 大
9a/76 62 34

RUI, tagu(i) – kind, type, genus

親類	*shinrui*	relative, kin	136
人類	*jinrui*	mankind	1
書類	*shorui*	papers, documents	70
分類	*bunrui*	classification	32

類

類 類 類

類 類 類

297 禾 車 一
5d/56 69 1

SHU – kind, type, seed **tane** – seed, species; cause

種類	*shurui*	kind, type, sort	296
一種	*isshu*	kind, sort	2
人種	*jinshu*	a human race	1
不安の種	*fuan no tane*	cause of unease	100, 105

種

種 種 種

種 種 種

298 亻 車 力
2a/3 69 8

DŌ, hatara(ku) – work

実働時間	*jitsudō jikan*	actual working hours	290, 34, 35
働き	*hataraki*	work; functioning; ability	
働き口	*hatarakiguchi*	job, position	87
働き者	*hatarakimono*	hard worker	129

働

働 働 働

働 働 働

299 龸 冂 力
3n/35 20 8

RŌ – labor, toil

労働	*rōdō*	work, labor	298
労働者	*rōdōsha*	worker, laborer	298, 129
労力	*rōryoku*	trouble, effort; labor	104
心労	*shinrō*	worry, concern	102

労

労 労 労

労 労 労

300

夂 一 力
4i/49 14 8

MU, tsuto(meru) – work, serve **tsuto(maru)** – be fit/competent for

事務所	*jimusho*	office	96, 270
公務員	*kōmuin*	government employee	113, 128
国務	*kokumu*	affairs of state	33
工務店	*kōmuten*	engineering firm	116, 133

務

務　務　務

務　務　務

301

氵 口 十
3a/21 24 12

KATSU – life, activity

生活	*seikatsu*	life	36
活発	*kappatsu*	active, lively	101
活動	*katsudō*	activity	156
活字	*katsuji*	printing/movable type	107

活

活　活　活

活　活　活

302

糸 土 冂
6a/61 22 20

ZOKU, tsuzu(ku) – (intr.) continue **tsuzu(keru)** – (tr.) continue

続出	*zokushutsu*	appear one after another	44
続行	*zokkō*	continuation	49
相続	*sōzoku*	succession; inheritance	266
手続き	*tetsuzuki*	procedures, formalities	89

続

続　続　続

続　続　続

303

亠 月 厶
2j/11 43 17

IKU, soda(tsu) – grow up **soda(teru), haguku(mu)** – raise

教育	*kyōiku*	education	160
体育	*taiiku*	physical education	91
発育	*hatsuiku*	growth, development	101
育ての親	*sodate no oya*	foster/adoptive parent	136

育

育　育　育

育　育　育

304

氵 亠 厶
3a/21 11 17

RYŪ – a current, style, school (of thought) **[RU], naga(reru)** – flow **naga(su)** – pour

流通	*ryūtsū*	circulation, distribution, ventilation	121
海流	*kairyū*	ocean current	109
流行	*ryūkō*	fashion, fad, popularity	49
一流	*ichiryū*	first class	2

305

艹 日 十
3k/32 42 12

SŌ, kusa – grass, plants

草原	*sōgen*	grassy plain, grasslands	264
草木	*sōmoku, kusaki*	plants and trees, vegetation	20
草本	*sōhon*	herb	23
草書	*sōsho*	(cursive script form of kanji)	70

306

艹 木 一
3k/32 41 1

YŌ, ha – leaf, foliage

葉書	*hagaki*	postcard	70
青葉	*aoba*	green foliage	145
言葉	*kotoba*	word; language	93
木の葉	*ko no ha*	tree leaves, foliage	20

307

亻 匕
2a/3 13

KA, KE, ba(keru) – turn oneself (into) **ba(kasu)** – bewitch

文化	*bunka*	culture	108
化学	*kagaku*	chemistry	65
強化	*kyōka*	strengthening	148
合理化	*gōrika*	rationalization, streamlining	272, 118

308	亠 夂 儿 2j/11 49 16	**HEN, ka(waru)** – (intr.) change **ka(eru)** – (tr.) change

変化　*henka*　change, alteration　307
変動　*hendō*　change, fluctuation　156
変種　*henshu*　variety, strain　297
変人　*henjin*　an eccentric　1

変

310	又 小 冂 2h/9 35 20	**JU, u(keru)** – receive, take (an exam) **u(karu)** – pass (an exam)

受理　*juri*　acceptance　118
受動　*judō*　passive　156
受け身　*ukemi*　passivity; passive (in grammar)　249
受け取る　*uketoru*　receive, accept, take　250

受

309	夂 心 小 4i/49 51 35	**AI** – love

愛情　*aijō*　love　291
愛国心　*aikokushin*　patriotic sentiment, patriotism　33, 102
愛読　*aidoku*　like to read　77
愛想　*aisō*　amiability, sociability　267

愛

311	戈 亠 4n/52 15	**SEI, [JŌ], na(ru)** – become, consist (of) **na(su)** – do, form

成長　*seichō*　growth　60
成年　*seinen*　(age of) majority, adulthood　37
成立　*seiritsu*　establishment, founding　111
成り行き　*nariyuki*　course (of events), development　49

成

312

心 戈 口
4k/51 52 24

KAN – feeling, sensation

五感	gokan	the five senses	7
感心	kanshin	admire	102
感想	kansō	one's thoughts, impressions	267
感情	kanjō	feelings, emotion	291

313

日 耳 又
4c/42 65 9

SAI, motto(mo) – highest, most

最後	saigo	end; last	39
最新	saishin	newest, latest	135
最大	saidai	maximum, greatest, largest	24
最高	saikō	maximum, highest, best	74

314

口 一
3d/24 14

GŌ – number; pseudonym

番号	bangō	(identification) number	280
三号室	sangōshitsu	Room No. 3	4, 131
年号	nengō	name/year of a reign era	37
信号	shingō	signal	271

315

土 十 丨
3b/22 12 2

ZAI – outskirts, country; be located **a(ru)** – be, exist

所在地	shozaichi	(prefectural) capital; (county) seat; location	270, 110
在日	zainichi	(stationed) in Japan	5
在外	zaigai	overseas, abroad	58
不在	fuzai	absence	100

316	子 十 丨
	2c/6 12 2

SON, ZON – exist; know, believe

存在	sonzai	existence	315
生存	seizon	existence, life	36
存続	sonzoku	continuance, duration	302
共存	kyōson	coexistence	284

317	一 耂 二
	0a 57 4

HYŌ – table, chart; surface; expression **omote** – surface, obverse **arawa(reru)** – be expressed

arawa(su) – express 34, 35

時間表	jikanhyō	timetable, schedule	
代表的	daihyōteki	representative, typical	165, 146
表情	hyōjō	facial expression	291
発表	happyō	announcement, publication	101

318	口 丆 几
	3s/24 14 16

MEN – face, mask, surface, aspect **omote, omo, tsura** – face

方面	hōmen	direction, side	94
表面	hyōmen	surface, exterior	317
面会	menkai	interview, meeting	125
面目	menmoku, menboku	face, honor, dignity	88

319	頁 口 几
	9a/76 24 16

TŌ, [TO], ZU, atama, kashira – head, leader, top

後頭（部）	kōtō(bu)	back of the head	39, 254
出頭	shuttō	appearance, attendance, presence	44
口頭	kōtō	oral, verbal	87
頭上	zujō	overhead	29

ᅠᅠᅠ

320 頁 立 彡
9a/76 54 31

GAN, kao – face

顔

顔面	ganmen	face	318
顔色	kaoiro	complexion; a look	142
新顔	shingao	stranger; newcomer	135
知らん顔	shirankao	pretend not to notice, ignore	147

321 立 土 宀
5b/54 22 15

SAN – childbirth; production; property **u(mu)** – give birth/rise to **u(mareru)** – be born **ubu** – birth; infant

産

出産	shussan	childbirth, delivery	44
生産	seisan	production	36
産物	sanbutsu	product	95
不動産	fudōsan	immovable property, real estate	100, 156

322 馬
10a/78

BA, uma, [ma] – horse

馬

馬車	basha	horse-drawn carriage	71
馬力	bariki	horsepower	104
馬術	bajutsu	horseback riding, dressage	281
馬小屋	umagoya	a stable	25, 132

323 言 王 戈
7a/67 46 52

GI – deliberation; proposal

議

会議	kaigi	conference, meeting	125
議会	gikai	parliament, Diet, congress	125
議員	giin	M.P., Dietman, congressman	128
不思議	fushigi	marvel, wonder, mystery	100, 103

324	言 艹 亻 7a/67 32 3	**RON** – discussion; argument, thesis, dissertation

論理	*ronri*	logic	118
理論	*riron*	theory	118
世論	*yoron, seron*	public opinion	163
論文	*ronbun*	thesis, essay	108

325	王 4f/46	**Ō** – king

王国	*ōkoku*	kingdom	33
国王	*kokuō*	king	33
女王	*joō*	queen	62
王子	*ōji*	prince	63

326	王 貝 4f/46 68	**GEN** – present *arawa(reru)* – appear *arawa(su)* – show

現代	*gendai*	contemporary, modern	165
現在	*genzai*	current, present; present tense	315
現金	*genkin*	cash	21
表現	*hyōgen*	an expression	317

327	丷 日 十 3n/35 42 12	**TAN** – single, simple; mono-

単語	*tango*	word	48
単位	*tan'i*	unit, denomination	261
単一	*tan'itsu*	single, simple, individual	2
単数	*tansū*	singular (in grammar)	295

328	戈 日 小
	4n/52 42 35

SEN, ikusa – war, battle **tataka(u)** – wage war, fight

内戦	naisen	civil war	253
交戦	kōsen	war, warfare	259
合戦	kassen	battle; contest	272
休戦	kyūsen	truce, cease-fire	45

329	〃 彐 丨
	2n/15 39 2

SŌ, araso(u) – dispute, argue, contend for

戦争	sensō	war	328
争議	sōgi	dispute, strife	323
論争	ronsō	dispute, controversy	324
言い争う	iiarasou	quarrel, argue	93

330	一 末 一
	0a 41 1

MATSU, BATSU, sue – end

週末	shūmatsu	weekend	99
月末	getsumatsu	end of the month	17
年末	nenmatsu	year's end	37
末っ子	suekko	youngest child	63

331	一 末 一
	0a 41 1

MI – not yet

未来	mirai	future	50
未知	michi	unknown	147
前代未聞	zendai mimon	unprecedented	38, 165, 47
未満	miman	less than, under	288

332

一 日 丨		
0a 42 2		

申

SHIN, mō(su) – say, be named

答申	*tōshin*	report, findings	126
上申	*jōshin*	report (to a superior)	29
内申	*naishin*	unofficial/confidential report	253
申し入れ	*mōshiire*	offer, proposal, notice	43

申 申 申

申 申 申

333

礻 日 丨		
4e/45 42 2		

神

SHIN, JIN, kami, [kan], [kō] – god, God

神道	*shintō*	Shintoism	120
神社	*jinja*	Shinto shrine	180
神話	*shinwa*	myth, mythology	76
神風	*kamikaze*	divine wind; kamikaze	83

神 神 神

神 神 神

334

一 大 ㇒		
0a 34 15		

失

SHITSU, ushina(u) – lose

失業	*shitsugyō*	unemployment	169
失意	*shitsui*	disappointment, despair	114
失神	*shisshin*	faint, lose consciousness	333
見失う	*miushinau*	lose sight of	46

失 失 失

失 失 失

335

一 大 一		
0a 34 1		

夫

FU, [FŪ], otto – husband

夫人	*fujin*	wife, Mrs.	1
人夫	*ninpu*	laborer	1
工夫	*kōfu*	laborer	116
工夫	*kufū*	contrivance	116

夫 夫 夫

夫 夫 夫

336

女 ヨ 巾
3e/25 39 26

FU – woman, wife

夫婦	*fūfu*	husband and wife, married couple	335
主婦	*shufu*	housewife	123
婦人	*fujin*	lady, woman	1
婦女（子）	*fujo(shi)*	woman	62, 63

婦

337

十 又
2k/12 9

SHI – branch; support **sasa(eru)** – support

支出	*shishutsu*	expenditure, disbursement	44
支社	*shisha*	branch (office)	180
支店	*shiten*	branch office/store	133
支流	*shiryū*	tributary (of a river)	304

支

338

禾 十 丶
5d/56 12 2

KA – academic course, department, faculty

科学	*kagaku*	science	65
理科	*rika*	natural sciences (department)	118
外科	*geka*	surgery	58
教科書	*kyōkasho*	textbook, schoolbook	160, 70

科

339

一 食
0a 77

RYŌ, yo(i) – good

良好	*ryōkō*	good, favorable, satisfactory	258
良質	*ryōshitsu*	good quality	137
最良	*sairyō*	best	313
不良	*furyō*	bad, unsatisfactory; delinquency	100

良

340	厂 又 2p/18 9

HAN, [HON] – anti- **[TAN]** – (unit of land/cloth measurement) **so(ru)** – (intr.) warp, bend back
so(rasu) – (tr.) warp, bend back

反発	*hanpatsu*	repulsion, repellence; opposition
反日	*han-Nichi*	anti-Japanese
反面	*hanmen*	the other side

101
5
318

341	宀 尸 冂 3m/33 40 20

KAN – government, authorities

半官半民	*hankan-hanmin*	semigovernmental
国務長官	*kokumu chōkan*	secretary of state
外交官	*gaikōkan*	diplomat
神官	*shinkan*	Shintō priest

59, 59, 276
33, 300, 60
58, 259
333

342	禾 刂 5d/56 16

RI – advantage, (loan) interest **ki(ku)** – take effect, work

有利	*yūri*	profitable, advantageous
利子	*rishi*	interest (on a loan)
利口	*rikō*	smart, clever, bright
左利き	*hidarikiki*	left-hander

166
63
87
55

343	亻 日 一 2a/3 42 14

BEN – convenience; excrement **BIN** – opportunity; mail **tayo(ri)** – news, tidings

便利	*benri*	convenient, handy
不便	*fuben*	inconvenient
便所	*benjo*	toilet
別便	*betsubin*	separate mail

342
100
270
167

344

亻 王
2a/3 46

NIN – duty, responsibility; office **maka(seru), maka(su)** – entrust (to)

主任	*shunin*	person in charge, manager, head	123
信任	*shinnin*	confidence, trust	271
後任	*kōnin*	successsor	39
任意	*nin'i*	optional, voluntary	114

任　任　任

任　任　任

345

木 隹 ⼍
4a/41 73 15

KEN, [GON] – authority, power, right

権利	*kenri*	a right	342
人権	*jinken*	human rights	1
特権	*tokken*	special right, privilege	172
三権分立	*sanken bunritsu*	separation of powers	4, 32, 111

権　権　権

権　権　権

346

言 月 口
7a/67 43 24

CHŌ, shira(beru) – investigate, check **totono(eru)** – prepare, arrange, put in order **totono(u)** – be prepared, arranged

好調	*kōchō*	good, favorable	258
調子	*chōshi*	tone; mood; condition	63
取り調べ	*torishirabe*	investigation, questioning	250

調　調　調

調　調　調

347

氵 日 宀
3a/21 42 33

EN – performance, play, presentation

上演	*jōen*	performance, dramatic presentation	29
公演	*kōen*	public performance	113
出演	*shutsuen*	appearance, performance	44
演出	*enshutsu*	production, staging (of a play)	44

演　演　演

演　演　演

348 糸 亻二
6a/61 3 4

KAI, E – picture

絵画	kaiga	pictures, paintings, drawings	191
絵葉書	ehagaki	picture postcard	306, 70
絵本	ehon	picture book	23
大和絵	Yamato-e	ancient Japanese-style painting	24, 263

349 糸 口 亻
6a/61 24 3

KYŪ – supply; salary

給料	kyūryō	pay, wages, salary	183
月給	gekkyū	monthly salary	17
支給	shikyū	supply, provision, allowance	337
供給	kyōkyū	supply	285

350 日 立
4c/42 54

AN, kura(i) – dark, dim

暗黒	ankoku	darkness	143
暗号	angō	(secret) code, cipher	314
明暗	meian	light and darkness, shading	81
暗がり	kuragari	darkness	

351 宀 疋 亻
3m/33 14 3

TEI, JŌ, sada(meru) – determine, decide **sada(maru)** – be determined, decided **sada(ka)** – certain, definite

安定	antei	stability, equilibrium	105
定食	teishoku	meal of fixed menu, combination meal, set menu	79
未定	mitei	undecided, unsettled, not yet fixed	331

352

氵 夬 一
3a/21　34　1

KETSU, ki(meru) – decide **ki(maru)** – be decided

決定	*kettei*	decision, determination	351
決心	*kesshin*	determination, resolution	102
決意	*ketsui*	determination, resolution	114
未決	*miketsu*	pending	331

353

艹 木 日
3k/32　41　42

YAKU, kusuri – medicine

薬学	*yakugaku*	pharmacy	65
薬品	*yakuhin*	medicine, drugs	155
薬味	*yakumi*	spices	179
薬屋	*kusuriya*	drugstore, pharmacy	132

354

日 亠 ト
4c/42　15　13

SAKU – past; yesterday

昨年	*sakunen*	last year	37
昨日	*sakujitsu, kinō*	yesterday	5
一昨日	*issakujitsu*	day before yesterday	2, 5
昨今	*sakkon*	these days, recent	42

355

几 又 厂
2s/20　9　18

DAN – step, stairs, rank; column

一段	*ichidan*	step; single-stage	2
石段	*ishidan*	stone stairway	252
手段	*shudan*	means, measure	89
段取り	*dandori*	program, plan, arrangements	250

356 — 由 ｜ 0a 42 2

YU, YŪ, [YUI], yoshi – reason, cause, significance

由来	*yurai*	origin, derivation	50
理由	*riyū*	reason, grounds	118
自由	*jiyū*	freedom	92
不自由	*fujiyū*	discomfort; want, privation	100, 92

357 — 対 2j/11 37 12

TAI – against　**TSUI** – pair

反対	*hantai*	opposite; opposition	340
対立	*tairitsu*	confrontation	111
対決	*taiketsu*	showdown	352
対面	*taimen*	interview, meeting	318

358 — 曲 儿 0a 42 16

KYOKU – curve; melody, musical composition　**ma(geru)** – bend, distort　**ma(garu)** – (intr.) bend, turn

作曲	*sakkyoku*	musical composition	198
楽曲	*gakkyoku*	musical composition/piece	197
名曲	*meikyoku*	famous/well-known melody	57
曲がり道	*magarimichi*	winding street	120

359 — 記 弓 7a/67 28

KI, shiru(su) – write/note down

記者	*kisha*	newsperson, journalist	129
記事	*kiji*	article, report	96
日記	*nikki*	diary	5
暗記	*anki*	memorize	350

360

彳 日 寸
3i/29 42 37

TOKU – profit, advantage **e(ru), u(ru)** – gain, acquire

所得	*shotoku*	income	270
得点	*tokuten*	one's score, points made	273
得意	*tokui*	prosperity; pride; one's strong point	114
心得る	*kokoroeru*	know, understand	102

得

361

彳 冂 又
3i/29 20 9

YAKU – service, use, office; post **EKI** – battle; service

役所	*yakusho*	government office/bureau	270
役目	*yakume*	one's duty, role	88
役者	*yakusha*	player, actor	129
使役	*shieki*	employment, service	187

役

362

舟 口 儿
6c/63 24 16

SEN, fune, [funa] – ship

船長	*senchō*	captain	60
船員	*sen'in*	crewman, seaman, sailor	128
船室	*senshitsu*	cabin	131
船旅	*funatabi*	sea voyage	151

船

363

氵 艹 厂
3a/21 32 18

TO, wata(ru) – cross **wata(su)** – hand over

渡し船	*watashibune*	ferryboat	362
渡り鳥	*wataridori*	migratory bird	174
見渡す	*miwatasu*	look out over	46
手渡す	*tewatasu*	hand deliver, hand over	89

渡

364	广 艹 巾 3q/18 32 26

SEKI – seat, place

出席	shusseki	attendance	44
満席	manseki	full, fully occupied	288
議席	giseki	seat (in parliament)	323
主席	shuseki	top seat, head, chief	123

席

365	欠 4j/49

KETSU, ka(ku) – lack **ka(keru)** – be lacking

欠点	ketten	defect, flaw	273
出欠	shukketsu	attendance (and/or absence)	44
欠席	kesseki	absence, nonattendance	364
欠員	ketsuin	vacant position, opening	128

欠

366	冫 欠 2b/5 49

JI, SHI, tsugi – next **tsu(gu)** – come/rank next

次男	jinan	second-oldest son	61
二次	niji	second, secondary	3
目次	mokuji	table of contents	88
相次ぐ	aitsugu	follow/happen one after another	266

次

367	耳 日 戈 6e/65 42 52

SHOKU – employment, job, occupation, office

職業	shokugyō	occupation, profession	169
職場	shokuba	place of work, jobsite	122
職員	shokuin	personnel, staff, staff member	128
現職	genshoku	one's present post	326

職

368 月 ム 宀 | 4b/43 17 13

NŌ – ability, function; Noh play

能力	nōryoku	capacity, talent	104
本能	honnō	instinct	23
能楽	nōgaku	Noh play	197
能面	nōmen	Noh mask	318

369 口 一 | 3d/24 14

KA – possible, -able

可能（性）	kanō(sei)	possibility	368, 257
不可能	fukanō	impossible	100, 368
不可欠	fukaketsu	indispensable, essential	100, 365
不可分	fukabun	indivisible	100, 32

370 一 了 一 | 0a 14 1

YO – in advance, previously

予約	yoyaku	subscription, reservation, booking	292
予定	yotei	plan; expectation	351
予想	yosō	expectation, supposition	267
予知	yochi	foresee, predict	147

371 彡 廾 一 | 3j/31 32 1

KEI, GYŌ, katachi, kata – form, shape

円形	enkei	round/circular shape	13
正方形	seihōkei	square	168, 94
人形	ningyō	doll, puppet	1
手形	tegata	(bank) bill, note, draft	89

372	門 十 丨 8e/75 12 2

HEI, shi(meru), to(jiru), to(zasu) – close, shut **shi(maru)** – become closed

開閉	kaihei	opening and closing	203
閉会	heikai	closing, adjournment	125
閉店	heiten	store closing	133
閉口	heikō	be dumbfounded	87

閉　閉　閉

373	門 大 儿 8e/75 34 16

KAN, seki – barrier **kaka(waru)** – be related (to), have to do (with)

関心	kanshin	interest	102
関東（地方）	Kantō (chihō)	(region including Tōkyō)	51, 110, 94
関西（地方）	Kansai (chihō)	(region including Ôsaka and Kyōto)	52, 110, 94
関所	sekisho	barrier station, checkpoint	270

関　関　関

374	言 口 儿 7a/67 24 16

SETSU – opinion, theory **ZEI, to(ku)** – explain, persuade

説明	setsumei	explanation	81
社説	shasetsu	an editorial	180
小説	shōsetsu	novel, story	25
演説	enzetsu	a speech	347

説　説　説

375	⸰ 王 大 2o/16 46 34

BI, utsuku(shii) – beautiful

美術館	bijutsukan	art museum/gallery	281, 186
美学	bigaku	esthetics	65
美人	bijin	beautiful woman	1
美化	bika	beautification	307

美　美　美

376

木 王 儿
4a/41 46 16

様

YŌ – way, manner; similarity; condition **sama** – condition **-sama** – Mr./Mrs./Miss …

様子	*yōsu* situation, aspect, appearance	63
同様	*dōyō* same; diversity, variety	141
神様	*kamisama* God	333
田中明様	*Tanaka Akira sama* Mr. Tanaka Akira	84, 26, 81

377

巾 尸 冂
3f/26 40 20

師

SHI – teacher; army

教師	*kyōshi* teacher, instructor	160
医師	*ishi* physician	149
法師	*hōshi* Buddhist priest	262
山師	*yamashi* speculator; adventurer; charlatan	31

378

亠 口 儿
2j/11 24 16

商

SHŌ, akina(u) – deal (in), trade

商人	*shōnin* merchant, dealer	1
商品	*shōhin* goods, merchandise	155
商業	*shōgyō* commerce, business	169
商売	*shōbai* trade, business; one's trade	158

379

辶 口 冂
2q/19 24 20

過

KA, su(giru) – pass, exceed; too much **su(gosu)** – spend (time) **ayama(tsu)** – err **ayama(chi)** – error

過度	*kado* excessive, too much	200
通過	*tsūka* passage, transit	121
過半数	*kahansū* majority, more than half	59, 295
食べ過ぎる	*tabesugiru* eat too much, overeat	79

380

适 口 亠
2q/19 24 11

適

TEKI – fit, be suitable

適当	*tekitō*	suitable, appropriate	251
適度	*tekido*	to a proper degree, moderate	200
適切	*tekisetsu*	pertinent, appropriate	85
適用	*tekiyō*	application (of a rule)	106

381

禾 王 口
5d/56 46 24

程

TEI, hodo – degree, extent

程度	*teido*	degree, extent, grade	200
過程	*katei*	a process	379
工程	*kōtei*	progress of the work; manufacturing process	116
日程	*nittei*	schedule for the day	5

382

糸 月 一
6a/61 43 1

組

SO, kumi – group, crew, class, gang **ku(mu)** – put together

組成	*sosei*	composition, makeup	311
番組	*bangumi*	(TV) program	280
労働組合	*rōdō kumiai*	labor union	299, 298, 272
組み合わせる	*kumiawaseru*	combine, fit together	272

383

女 口 一
3e/25 24 14

要

YŌ – main point, necessity **i(ru)** – need, be necessary **kaname** – pivot; main point

重要	*jūyō*	important	153
主要	*shuyō*	principal, major	123
要点	*yōten*	main point(s), gist	273
要約	*yōyaku*	summary	292

384 目 儿 一
5c/55 16 1

GU – tool, equipment, gear

具体的　*gutaiteki*　concrete, specific　　91, 146
道具　*dōgu*　tool, implement　　120
家具　*kagu*　furniture　　130
金具　*kanagu*　metal fitting　　21

具　具　具

具　具　具

385 十 目 丨
2k/12 55 2

CHOKU, JIKI – honest, frank, direct **nao(su)** – fix, correct **nao(ru)** – be fixed, corrected

直前　*chokuzen*　immediately before　　*tada(chi ni)* – immediately　38
直後　*chokugo*　immediately after　　39
正直　*shōjiki*　honest, upright　　168
書き直す　*kakinaosu*　write over again, rewrite　　70

直　直　直

直　直　直

386 亻 目 十
2a/3 55 12

CHI, ne, atai – value, price

値うち　*neuchi*　value; public estimation
値段　*nedan*　price　　355
値上げ　*neage*　price increase　　29
値切る　*negiru*　haggle over the price, bargain　　85

値　値　値

値　値　値

387 罒 十 丨
5g/55 12 2

CHI, o(ku) – put, set, leave behind, leave as is

位置　*ichi*　position, location　　261
置き物　*okimono*　ornament; figurehead　　95
物置き　*monooki*　storeroom, shed　　95
前置き　*maeoki*　introductory remarks, preface　　38

置　置　置

置　置　置

388	刂 牛 冂 2f/16 47 20	**SEI** – system; regulations	
		制度 *seido* system	200
		体制 *taisei* structure, system, order; the establishment	91
		新制 *shinsei* new order, reorganization	135
		強制 *kyōsei* compulsion, force	148

389	彳 土 卜 3i/29 22 13	**TO** – on foot; companions; vain, useless	
		生徒 *seito* pupil, student	36
		徒歩 *toho* walking	211
		徒手 *toshu* empty-handed; penniless	89
		徒労 *torō* vain effort	299

390	亻 二 厶 2a/3 4 17	**DEN, tsuta(eru)** – transmit, impart **tsuta(waru)** – be transmitted, imparted **tsuta(u)** – go along	
		伝記 *denki* biography	359
		伝説 *densetsu* legend, folklore	374
		伝道 *dendō* evangelism, missionary work	120
		手伝い *tetsudai* help, helper	89

391	辶 隹 2q/19 73	**SHIN, susu(mu)** – advance, progress **susu(meru)** – advance, promote	
		進歩 *shinpo* progress, improvement	211
		進行 *shinkō* progress, onward movement	49
		進学 *shingaku* entrance to a higher school	65
		先進国 *senshinkoku* developed/advanced country	41, 33

392 辶 車
2q/19 69

REN – group; accompaniment **tsu(reru)** – take (someone) along **tsura(naru)** – stand in a row

連続　*renzoku*　series, continuity

連合　*rengō*　combination, league, coalition

国連　*Kokuren*　UN, United Nations

家族連れ　*kazokuzure*　with the family

⌊*tsura(neru)* – link, put in a row　302

272

33

130, 150

連　連　連

連　連　連

393 辶 厂 又
2q/19 18 9

HEN, kae(su) – (tr.) return **kae(ru)** – (itr.) return

返事　*henji*　reply　96

返信　*henshin*　reply (letter, email)　271

見返す　*mikaesu*　look back; triumph over (an old enemy)　46

読み返す　*yomikaesu*　reread　77

返　返　返

返　返　返

394 阝 厂 又
2d/7 18 9

HAN – slope; embankment

大阪　*Ōsaka*　Ōsaka　24

京阪　*Kei-Han*　Kyōto-Ōsaka (area)　140

阪神　*Han-Shin*　Ōsaka-Kōbe (area)　333

京阪神　*Kei-Han-Shin*　Kyōto-Ōsaka-Kōbe (area)　140, 333

阪　阪　阪

阪　阪　阪

395 辶 衤 土
2q/19 57 22

EN, [ON], tō(i) – far, distant

遠方　*enpō*　great distance, (in) the distance　94

遠近法　*enkinhō*　(law of) perspective　216, 262

遠足　*ensoku*　excursion, outing　90

遠回し　*tōmawashi*　indirect, roundabout　256

遠　遠　遠

遠　遠　遠

396	口 衤 土 3s/24 57 22	**EN, sono** – garden	

公園	kōen	(public) park	113
動物園	dōbutsuen	zoo	156, 95
学園	gakuen	educational institution, academy	65
楽園	rakuen	paradise	197

397	辶 王 土 2q/19 46 22	**TATSU** – reach, arrive at	

上達	jōtatsu	progress; proficiency	29
発達	hattatsu	development	101
達人	tatsujin	expert, master	1
友達	tomodachi	friend	78

398	月 艹 二 4b/43 32 4	**KI, [GO]** – time, period, term	

期間	kikan	period of time, term	35
定期	teiki	fixed period	351
過渡期	katoki	transition period	379, 363
学期	gakki	semester, trimester, school term	65

399	扌 口 力 3c/23 24 8	**SHŌ, mane(ku)** – beckon to, invite, cause	

招待	shōtai	invitation	218
招待席	shōtaiseki	reserved seats for guests	218, 364
手招き	temaneki	beckoning	89

400
3m/33 32 4

KAN – cold; midwinter ***samu(i)*** – cold

寒気	*kanki*	the cold	72
寒中	*kanchū*	the cold season	26
寒流	*kanryū*	cold current	304
寒空	*samuzora*	wintry sky, cold weather	117

401
4g/47 43 15

KAI, GE, to(ku) – untie, solve ***to(keru)*** – come loose, be solved ***to(kasu)*** – comb

理解	*rikai*	understanding	118
解説	*kaisetsu*	explanation, commentary	374
解決	*kaiketsu*	solution, settlement	352
和解	*wakai*	compromise	263

402
6b/62 13 11

SHI, ha – tooth

歯科医	*shikai*	dentist	338, 149
歯医者	*haisha*	dentist	149, 129
歯ブラシ	*haburashi*	toothbrush	
歯車	*haguruma*	toothed wheel, gear	71

403
4n/52 35 13

SAI – year, years old **[SEI]** – year

満四歳	*man'yonsai*	4 (full) years old	288, 6
２０歳	*hatachi*	20 years old	
万歳	*banzai*	Hurrah! Long live ... !	16
歳入歳出	*sainyū saishutsu*	yearly revenue and expenditure	43, 44

404

夂 ユ 一
4i/49 38 1

SEI, [SHŌ], matsurigoto – government, rule

政局	seikyoku	political situation	274
行政	gyōsei	administration	49
内政	naisei	domestic politics, internal affairs	253
家政	kasei	management of a household, housekeeping	130

政

政 政 政

政 政 政

405

一 日 木
0a 42 41

KA – fruit, result **ha(tasu)** – carry out, complete **ha(teru)** – come to an end **ha(te)** – end; limit; result

果実	kajitsu	fruit	290
青果（物）	seika(butsu)	vegetables and fruits	145, 95
成果	seika	result	311
果物	kudamono	fruit	95

果

果 果 果

果 果 果

406

宀 寸
3m/33 37

SHU, [SU], mamo(ru) – protect; obey, abide by **mori** – babysitter; (lighthouse) keeper

死守	shishu	desperately fought defense	98
子守	komori	baby-sitting; baby-sitter, nursemaid	63
見守る	mimamoru	keep watch over; stare at	46
お守り	omamori	charm, amulet	

守

守 守 守

守 守 守

407

氵 口 厶
3a/21 24 17

JI, CHI – peace; government; healing **osa(meru)** – govern; suppress **osa(maru)** – be at peace; quelled **nao(su)** – (tr.) heal **nao(ru)** – (intr.) heal

政治	seiji	politics	404
自治	jichi	self-government, autonomy	92
明治時代	Meiji jidai	Meiji era (1868-1912)	81, 34, 165

治

治 治 治

治 治 治

408 | 3n/35 24 26

常

JŌ, tsune – normal, usual, continual **toko-** – ever-, always

日常生活	*nichijō seikatsu*	everyday life	5, 36, 301
常用漢字	*jōyō kanji*	kanji for general use	106, 236, 107
正常	*seijō*	normal	168
常務	*jōmu*	regular business, routine duties	300

常 常 常

常 常 常

---

409 | 0a 4 13

非

HI – mistake; (prefix) non-, un-

非常口	*hijōguchi*	emergency exit	408, 87
非公開	*hikōkai*	not open to the public, private	113, 203
非人間的	*hiningenteki*	inhuman, impersonal	1, 35, 146
非合法	*higōhō*	illegal	272, 262

非 非 非

非 非 非

---

410 | 0a 41 24

束

SOKU, taba – bundle, sheaf

一束	*issoku, hitotaba*	a bundle	2
約束	*yakusoku*	promise, appointment	292
花束	*hanataba*	bouquet	164
束ねる	*tabaneru*	tie in a bundle; control	

束 束 束

束 束 束

---

411 | 2q/19 41 24

速

SOKU, haya(i), sumi(yaka) – fast, speedy **haya(meru)** – hasten, expedite **haya(maru)** – speed up, gather speed

速力、速度	*sokuryoku, sokudo*	speed, velocity	104, 200
高速道路	*kōsoku dōro*	expressway, freeway	74, 120, 269
速達	*sokutatsu*	special/express delivery	397
速記	*sokki*	shorthand, stenography	359

速 速 速

速 速 速

412

月 火 二
4b/43 44   4

勝

SHŌ, ka(tsu) – win **masa(ru)** – be superior (to)

勝利	shōri	victory	342
勝（利）者	shō(ri)sha	victor, winner	342, 129
決勝	kesshō	decision (of a competition)	352
勝ち通す	kachitōsu	win successive victories	121

413

ク 貝
2n/15 68

負

FU, ma(keru) – be defeated, lose; give a discount **ma(kasu)** – beat, defeat **o(u)** – carry, bear, owe

勝負	shōbu	victory or defeat; game, match	412
自負	jifu	conceit, self-importance	92
負けん気	makenki	unyielding/competitive spirit	72
負け犬	makeinu	loser	170

414

貝 攵
7b/68 49

敗

HAI – a defeat **yabu(reru)** – be defeated

敗北	haiboku	defeat	53
勝敗	shōhai	victory or defeat, outcome	412
失敗	shippai	failure, blunder	334
敗戦	haisen	lost battle, defeat	328

415

方 攵
4h/48 49

放

HŌ, hana(tsu) – set free, release; fire (a gun); emit **hana(su)** – set free, release **hana(reru)** – get free of **hō(ru)** – throw; leave as is

解放	kaihō	liberation, emancipation	401
放送	hōsō	(radio/TV) broadcasting	215
放火	hōka	arson	18

416 酉 弓 7e/71 28

HAI, kuba(ru) – distribute, pass out

心配	shinpai	worry, concern	102
支配	shihai	management, administration, rule	337
配達	haitatsu	deliver	397
気配	kehai	sign, indication	72

配

---

417 氵 酉 3a/21 71

SHU, sake, [saka] – saké, rice wine, liquor

日本酒	Nihon-shu	saké, Japanese rice wine	5, 23
ぶどう酒	budōshu	(grape) wine	
酒屋	sakaya	wine dealer, liquor store	132
酒場	sakaba	bar, saloon, tavern	122

酒

---

418 宀 士 口 3m/33 22 24

GAI – injury, harm, damage

公害	kōgai	pollution	113
水害	suigai	flood damage, flooding	19
利害	rigai	advantages and disadvantages	342
有害	yūgai	harmful, noxious, injurious	166

害

---

419 刂 宀 士 2f/16 33 22

KATSU, wa(ru) – divide, separate, split **wa(reru)** – break, crack/split apart **wari** – proportion; profit; 10 percent **sa(ku)** – cut up, separate; spare (time)

分割	bunkatsu	division, partitioning	32
割合	wariai	rate, proportion; percentage	272
割引	waribiki	discount	293

割

420	一 必 丨 0a 51 2	**HITSU, kanara(zu)** – surely, (be) sure (to), without fail

必 | 必要 | hitsuyō | necessary, requisite | 383
必死 | hisshi | certain death; desperation | 98
必読 | hitsudoku | required reading | 77
必勝 | hisshō | sure victory | 412

421	一 禾 丿 0a 41 32	**JŌ, no(ru)** – get in/on, ride, take (a train); be fooled **no(seru)** – take aboard; deceive, take in

乗 | 乗用車 | jōyōsha | passenger car | 106, 71
大乗的 | daijōteki | broad-minded | 24, 146
乗組員 | norikumiin | (ship's) crew | 382, 128
乗っ取る | nottoru | take over, commandeer, hijack | 250

422	弋 工 4n/52 38	**SHIKI** – ceremony, rite; style, form; method; formula

式 | 正式 | seishiki | prescribed form, formal | 168
公式 | kōshiki | formula (in mathematics); formal, official | 113
様式 | yōshiki | mode, style | 376
方式 | hōshiki | formula, mode; method, system | 94

423	木 弋 厶 4a/41 52 17	**KI** – machine; opportunity **hata** – loom

機 | 機関 | kikan | engine; machinery, organ, medium | 373
制動機 | seidōki | a brake | 388, 156
機能 | kinō | a function | 368
機会 | kikai | opportunity, occasion, chance | 125

424	一 乀 十
	0a 10 12

HI, to(bu) – fly **to(basu)** – let fly, skip over, omit

飛行　*hikō*　flight, aviation　49
飛行機　*hikōki*　airplane　49, 423
飛行場　*hikōjō*　airport　49, 122
飛び石　*tobiishi*　stepping-stones　252

425	阝 口 亻
	2d/7 24 3

KEN, kewa(shii) – steep, inaccessible; stern, harsh

険悪　*ken'aku*　dangerous, threatening　178
険路　*kenro*　steep path　269
険しい道　*kewashii michi*　steep/treacherous road　120
険しい顔つき　*kewashii kaotsuki*　stern/fierce look　320

426	ク 厂 阝
	2n/15 18 7

KI, abu(nai), aya(ui) – dangerous **aya(bumu)** – fear

危険　*kiken*　danger　425
危険物　*kikenbutsu*　hazardous articles　425, 95
危機　*kiki*　crisis, critical moment　423
危急　*kikyū*　emergency, crisis　177

427	扌 木 冂
	3c/23 41 20

TAN, sagu(ru) – search/grope for **saga(su)** – look for

探知　*tanchi*　detection　147
探り出す　*saguridasu*　spy/sniff out (a secret)　44
探し回る　*sagashimawaru*　look/search around for　256
家探し　*iesagashi*　house hunting　130

428	氵 木 冂
	3a/21 41 20

SHIN, fuka(i) – deep **fuka(meru)** – make deeper, intensify **fuka(maru)** – become deeper, intensify

深度	shindo	depth, deepness	200
深夜	shin'ya	dead of night, late at night	227
情け深い	nasakebukai	compassionate, merciful	291
用心深い	yōjinbukai	careful, cautious, wary	106, 102

深

深 深 深

深 深 深

429	一 十 一
	0a 12 1

YO – give; participate in **ata(eru)** – give, grant

給与	kyūyo	allowance, wage	349
付与	fuyo	give, grant, confer	283
与信	yoshin	granting/extending credit, lending	271
関与	kan'yo	participation	373

与

与 与 与

与 与 与

430	十 土 十
	2k 22 13

RŌ – old age **o(iru), fu(keru)** – grow old

老人	rōjin	old man/woman/people	1
長老	chōrō	an elder	60
老夫婦	rōfūfu	old married couple	335, 336
海老	ebi	shrimp, prawn	109

老

老 老 老

老 老 老

431	艹 口 十
	3k/32 24 12

JAKU, [NYAKU], waka(i) – young **mo(shikuwa)** – or

老若	rōnyaku, rōjaku	young and old, youth and age	430
若者	wakamono	young man/people	129
若手	wakate	young man, a younger member	89
若人	wakōdo	young man, a youth	1

若

若 若 若

若 若 若

432

十 冂 十
3k/32 24 12

KU – pain, suffering(s) **kuru(shimu)** – suffer **kuru(shimeru)** – torment **kuru(shii)** – painful

			niga(i) – bitter **niga(ru)** – scowl	299
苦労	kurō	trouble, hardship, adversity		
苦心	kushin	pains, efforts		102
病苦	byōku	the pain of illness		201
重苦しい	omokurushii	oppressed, gloomy, ponderous		153

苦

苦 苦 苦

苦 苦 苦

433

糸 土 又
6a/61 22 9

KEI – longitude; sutra; passage of time **KYŌ** – sutra **he(ru)** – pass, elapse

経験	keiken	experience	233
経理	keiri	accounting	118
神経	shinkei	a nerve	333
月経	gekkei	menstruation	17

経

経 経 経

経 経 経

434

氵 宀 十
3a/21 11 12

SAI, su(mu) – come to an end; be paid; suffice **su(masu)** – finish, settle; pay; make do, manage

経済	keizai	economy, economics	433
返済	hensai	payment, repayment	393
決済	kessai	settlement of accounts	352
使用済み	shiyōzumi	used up	187, 106

済

済 済 済

済 済 済

435

一 十 亅
0a 12 2

SAI – ability, talent; (as suffix) years old

天才	tensai	a genius	73
才子	saishi	talented person	63
才能	sainō	talent, ability	368
十八才	jūhassai	18 years old	12, 10

才

才 才 才

才 才 才

436

貝 十 一
7b/68 12 2

ZAI, [SAI] – money, wealth, property

財産	*zaisan*	estate, assets, property		321
財政	*zaisei*	finances, financial affairs		404
財界	*zaikai*	financial world, business circles		219
文化財	*bunkazai*	cultural asset		108, 307

437

囗 大
3s/24 34

IN – cause **yo(ru)** – depend (on), be limited (to)

原因	*gen'in*	cause	264
主因	*shuin*	primary/main cause	123
死因	*shiin*	cause of death	98
因果	*inga*	cause and effect	405

438

隹 艹 口
8c/73 32 24

NAN, muzuka(shii), kata(i) – difficult

難題	*nandai*	difficult problem/question	195
難病	*nanbyō*	incurable disease	201
難民	*nanmin*	refugees	276
海難	*kainan*	disaster at sea, shipwreck	109

439

囗 木
3s/24 41

KON, koma(ru) – be distressed, be troubled

困難	*konnan*	difficulty, trouble	438
困苦	*konku*	hardships, adversity	432
困り切る	*komarikiru*	be in a bad fix, at a loss	85
困り果てる	*komarihateru*	be greatly troubled, nonplussed	405

440

力 艹 口
2g/8 32 24

勤

KIN – service, work **[GON]** – Buddhist religious services **tsuto(meru)** – be employed

勤労　kinrō　work, labor 299
勤務　kinmu　service, being on duty/at work 300
通勤　tsūkin　going to work, commuting 121
勤め先　tsutomesaki　place of work, employer 41

tsuto(maru) – be fit for 299

441

女 日 厂
3e/25 42 18

婚

KON – marriage

婚約　kon'yaku　engagement 292
新婚旅行　shinkon ryokō　honeymoon 135, 151, 49
金婚式　kinkonshiki　golden wedding anniversary 21, 422
未婚　mikon　unmarried 331

442

⺮ 土 寸
6f/66 22 37

等

TŌ – class, grade; equality; etc. **hito(shii)** – equal

一等　ittō　first class 2
平等　byōdō　equality 289
同等　dōtō　equality, same rank 141
高等学校　kōtō gakkō　senior high school 74, 65, 68

443

隹 木 十
8c/73 41 12

雑

ZATSU, ZŌ – miscellany, a mix

雑音　zatsuon　noise, static 192
雑感　zakkan　miscellaneous thoughts/impressions 312
雑学　zatsugaku　knowledge of various subjects 65
雑草　zassō　weeds 305

444	木 十 冂 4a/41　12　20	**SATSU, [SETSU], koro(su)** – kill **[SAI]** – lessen	

自殺	*jisatsu*	suicide	92
暗殺	*ansatsu*	assassination	350
殺人	*satsujin*	a murder	1
人殺し	*hitogoroshi*	murder; murderer	1

殺 | 殺 | 殺 | 殺

殺 | 殺 | 殺

445	亻 口 阝 2a/3　24　7	**MEI** – command, fate, life **MYŌ, inochi** – life	

生命	*seimei*	life	36
運命	*unmei*	fate	214
使命	*shimei*	mission, errand	187
任命	*ninmei*	appointment, nomination	344

命 | 命 | 命 | 命

命 | 命 | 命

446	亻 心 一 2a/3　51　1	**NEN** – thought, idea; desire; concern, attention	

記念日	*kinenbi*	memorial day, anniversary	359, 5
理念	*rinen*	idea, doctrine, ideology	118
信念	*shinnen*	belief, faith, conviction	271
念入り	*nen'iri*	careful, scrupulous, thorough	43

念 | 念 | 念 | 念

念 | 念 | 念

447	頁 日 小 9a/76　42　35	**GAN, nega(u)** – petition, request, desire	

大願	*taigan*	great ambition, earnest wish	24
念願	*nengan*	one's heart's desire	446
出願	*shutsugan*	application	44
願書	*gansho*	written request, application	70

願 | 願 | 願 | 願

願 | 願 | 願

448	扌 厶 3c/23 17	**FUTSU, hara(u)** – pay; sweep away	
		支払い *shiharai* payment	337
		前払い *maebarai* payment in advance	38
		現金払い *genkinbarai* cash payment	326, 21
		分割払い *bunkatsubarai* payment in installments	32, 419

払　払　払

449	日 匕 丨 4c/42 13 2	**KAI, mina** – all	
		皆済 *kaisai* payment in full	434
		皆勤 *kaikin* perfect attendance (at work/school)	440
		皆目 *kaimoku* utterly; (not) at all	88
		皆さん *minasan* everybody; Ladies and Gentlemen	

皆　皆　皆

450	言 火 7a/67 44	**DAN** – conversation	
		会談 *kaidan* a conversation, conference	125
		対談 *taidan* face-to-face talk, conversation	357
		談話 *danwa* conversation	76
		相談 *sōdan* consultation	266

談　談　談

451	石 隹 冂 5a/53 73 20	**KAKU, tashi(ka)** – certain **tashi(kameru)** – make sure of, verify	
		確立 *kakuritsu* establishment, settlement	111
		確定 *kakutei* decision, settlement	351
		確実 *kakujitsu* certain, reliable	290
		確信 *kakushin* firm belief, conviction	271

確　確　確

452 — 催 貝 宀 (73 68 15)

KAN – appearance, view

観光	kankō	sight-seeing, tourism	265
外観	gaikan	(external) appearance	58
主観的	shukanteki	subjective	123, 146
楽観的	rakkanteki	optimistic	197, 146

観　観　観

観　観　観

453 — ⺌ 貝 冖 (3n/35 68 20)

KAKU, obo(eru) – remember, bear in mind; learn; feel **sa(meru), sa(masu)** – (intr./tr.) awake, wake up

感覚	kankaku	sense, sensation, feeling	312
味覚	mikaku	sense of taste	179
見覚え	mioboe	recognition, knowing by sight	46
目覚まし（時計）	mezamashi(dokei)	alarm clock	88, 34, 190

覚　覚　覚

覚　覚　覚

454 — 目 貝 夫 (5c 68 34)

KI – standard, measure

規定	kitei	stipulations, provisions, regulations	351
定規	jōgi	ruler, square; standard, norm	351
正規	seiki	regular, normal, formal, legal	168
新規	shinki	new	135

規　規　規

規　規　規

455 — 亻 貝 儿 (2a/3 68 16)

SOKU, gawa – side

側面	sokumen	side, flank	318
側近	sokkin	close associate, those close to (the Prime Minister)	216
左側	hidarigawa	left side	55
反対側	hantaigawa	opposite side	340, 357

側　側　側

側　側　側

456

刂 夕 一
2f/16 30 1

RETSU – row

列車	ressha	train	71
列国	rekkoku	world powers, nations	33
行列	gyōretsu	queue; procession; matrix	49
前列／後列	zenretsu / kōretsu	front row / back row	38, 39

457

亻 夕 儿
2a/3 30 16

REI – example; custom, precedent **tato(eru)** – compare

例外	reigai	exception	58
特例	tokurei	special case, exception	172
先例	senrei	previous example, precedent	41
例年	reinen	normal year; every year	37

458

宀 二 儿
3m/33 4 16

KAN – completion

完全	kanzen	complete, perfect	255
完成	kansei	completion, accomplishment	311
未完成	mikansei	incomplete, unfinished	331, 311
完敗	kanpai	complete defeat	414

459

礻
4e/45

JI, SHI, shime(su) – show

公示	kōji	public announcement	113
明示	meiji	clear statement	81
教示	kyōji	instruction, teaching	160
暗示	anji	hint, suggestion	350

460	阝 ネ 夕 2d/7 45 30	**SAI** – time, occasion **kiwa** – side, brink, edge

際

国際　kokusai　international 33
交際　kōsai　association, company, acquaintance 259
実際　jissai　truth, reality, actual practice 290
際立つ　kiwadatsu　be conspicuous, stand out 111

461	宀 ネ 夕 3m/33 45 30	**SATSU** – surmise, judge, understand, sympathize

察

観察　kansatsu　observation 452
観察力　kansatsuryoku　power of observation 452, 104
考察　kōsatsu　consideration, examination 235
明察　meisatsu　discernment, keen insight 81

462	ネ | 4e/45 2	**REI, RAI** – courtesy; salutation; gratitude, remuneration

礼

礼式　reishiki　etiquette 422
返礼　henrei　return gift, in return for 393
失礼　shitsurei　rudeness 334
非礼　hirei　impoliteness 409

463	ネ 月 一 4e/45 43 1	**SO** – ancestor

祖

祖先　sosen　ancestor, forefather 41
祖母／祖父　sobo／sofu　grandmother / grandfather 66, 67
祖国　sokoku　one's homeland/fatherland 33
元祖　ganso　originator, founder, inventor 115

464
力 月 |
2g/8 43 2

JO, tasu(keru) – help, rescue **tasu(karu)** – be helped, rescued **suke** – assistance

助力	joryoku	help, assistance
助言	jogen	advice
助手	joshu	helper, assistant
助け合う	tasukeau	help each other

104
93
89
272

465
冫 犭 |
2b/5 27 2

JŌ – condition, circumstances; form; letter

現状	genjō	present situation
白状	hakujō	confession
礼状	reijō	letter of thanks
招待状	shōtaijō	written invitation

326
75
462
399, 218

466
一 大 丶
0a 34 2

TAI, TA – big **futo(i)** – fat **futo(ru)** – get fat

太平洋	Taiheiyō	Pacific Ocean
太古	taiko	antiquity, prehistoric times
与太者	yotamono	a good-for-nothing
太字	futoji	thick character, boldface

289, 175
134
429, 129
107

467
阝 日 勿
2d/7 42 27

YŌ – Yang principle; active; positive; sun

太陽	taiyō	sun
陽光	yōkō	sunshine, sunlight
陽気	yōki	season, weather; cheerfulness, gaiety
陽性	yōsei	positive

466
265
72
257

468　宀夂口　3m/33　49　24

KYAKU, KAKU – guest, customer

来客	*raikyaku*	visitor, caller	50
乗客	*jōkyaku*	passenger	421
客観的	*kyakkanteki*	objective	452, 146
旅客	*ryokaku*	passender, traveler	151

客　客　客

客 客 客

469　木夂口　4a/41　49　24

KAKU, [KŌ] – status, rank; standard, rule; case

人格	*jinkaku*	personality, character	1
性格	*seikaku*	character, personality	257
合格	*gōkaku*	pass (an exam)	272
格子	*kōshi*	lattice, bars, grating, grille	63

格　格　格

格 格 格

470　火土几　4d/44　22　16

NETSU – heat, fever **atsu(i)** – hot (object)

熱病	*netsubyō*	fever	201
高熱	*kōnetsu*	high fever	74
情熱	*jōnetsu*	passion	291
熱心	*nesshin*	enthusiasm, zeal	102

熱　熱　熱

熱 熱 熱

471　一戈夕　0a　52　30

ZAN, noko(ru) – remain **noko(su)** – leave behind

残念	*zannen*	regret, disappointment; too bad	446
残業	*zangyō*	overtime	169
残高	*zandaka*	balance, remainder	74
残り物	*nokorimono*	leftovers	95

残　残　残

残 残 残

472	火 夕 犭 4d/44 30 27	**ZEN, NEN** – as, like

全然	zenzen	(not) at all; completely	255
当然	tōzen	naturally, (as a matter) of course	251
自然	shizen	nature	92
天然	tennen	natural	73

473	宀 火 口 3m/33 44 24	**YŌ** – form, appearance; content

美容院	biyōin	beauty parlor, hairdresser's	375, 238
形容	keiyō	form, appearance; modify; metaphor	371
内容	naiyō	content	253
変容	hen'yō	changed appearance, metamorphosis	308

474	貝 土 一 7b/68 22 1	**SEKI** – responsibility; censure **se(meru)** – condemn, censure; torture

責任	sekinin	responsibility	344
重責	jūseki	heavy responsibility	153
責務	sekimu	duty, obligation	300
自責	jiseki	self-reproach, pangs of conscience	92

475	禾 貝 土 5d/56 68 22	**SEKI** – accumulation; product (in math); size, volume **tsu(moru)** – be piled up, accumulate

面積	menseki	(surface) area	⌐tsu(mu) – heap up, load	318
見積（書）	mitsumori(sho)	(written) estimate		46, 70
積み重ねる	tsumikasaneru	stack up one on another		153
下積み	shitazumi	goods piled underneath; lowest social classes		28

476

2o/16 46 38

差

SA – difference **sa(su)** – hold (an umbrella), wear (a sword), offer (a cup of saké)

時差	*jisa*	time difference/lag	34
差別	*sabetsu*	discrimination	167
交差点	*kōsaten*	intersection	259, 273
差し支え	*sashitsukae*	impediment; objection	337

差　差　差

差　差　差

477

6b/62 43 22

精

SEI, [SHŌ] – spirit; energy, vitality

精力	*seiryoku*	energy, vigor, vitality	104
精神	*seishin*	mind, spirit	333
精進	*shōjin*	diligence, devotion; purification	391
不精	*bushō*	sloth, laziness, indolence	100

精　精　精

精　精　精

478

4c/42 43 22

晴

SEI – clear **ha(reru)** – (intr.) clear up **ha(rasu)** – (tr.) clear up

晴天	*seiten*	clear sky, fine weather	73
秋晴れ	*akibare*	clear autumn weather	224
見晴らし	*miharashi*	view, vista	46
気晴らし	*kibarashi*	pastime, diversion	72

晴　晴　晴

晴　晴　晴

479

4b/43 22 39

静

SEI, [JŌ], shizu, shizu(ka) – quiet, peaceful, still **shizu(meru)** – make peaceful

静物	*seibutsu*	still life	⌐*shizu(maru)* – become peaceful 95
静止	*seishi*	stillness, rest, stationary	228
安静	*ansei*	rest, quiet, repose	105
平静	*heisei*	calm, serenity	289

静　静　静

静　静　静

480

石 厂 又
5a/53 18 9

HA, yabu(ru) – tear, break **yabu(reru)** – get torn/broken

破産	*hasan*	bankruptcy	321
破局	*hakyoku*	catastrophe, ruin	274
破約	*hayaku*	breach of contract/promise	292
破れ目	*yabureme*	a tear, split	88

破

破 破 破

破 破 破

481

氵 艹 弓
3a/21 32 28

KŌ, minato – harbor, port

空港	*kūkō*	airport	117
内向	*naikō*	inner harbor	253, 286
港内	*kōnai*	in the harbor	253
港町	*minatomachi*	port city	139

港

港 港 港

港 港 港

482

女 彐 十
3e/25 39 12

SAI, tsuma – wife

夫妻	*fusai*	husband and wife, Mr. and Mrs.	335
妻子	*saishi*	wife and child/children, family	63
後妻	*gosai*	second wife	39
良妻	*ryōsai*	good wife	339

妻

妻 妻 妻

妻 妻 妻

483

亠 丨
2j/11 2

BŌ, [MŌ] – die **na(i)** – dead, deceased

死亡者	*shibōsha*	the dead	98, 129
亡父	*bōfu*	one's late father	67
亡夫	*bōfu*	one's late husband	335
未亡人	*mibōjin*	widow	331, 1

亡

亡 亡 亡

亡 亡 亡

484

王 夕 亠
4f/46 30 11

BŌ, MŌ, nozo(mu) – desire, wish, hope for

宿望	shukubō	long-cherished desire	278
要望	yōbō	demand, wish	383
失望	shitsubō	despair, disappointment	334
大望	taimō	great desire, ambition	24

望

485

衤 刀
5e/57 8

SHO – first; beginning **haji(me)** – beginning **haji(mete)** – for the first time **hatsu-, ui-** – first

最初	saisho	beginning, first	⌐**-so(meru)** – begin to 313
初心者	shoshinsha	beginner	102, 129
初歩	shoho	rudiments, ABCs	211
初耳	hatsumimi	something heard for the first time	248

初

486

言 戈 日
7a/67 52 42

SHIKI – know; discriminate

意識	ishiki	consciousness	114
知識	chishiki	knowledge	147
常識	jōshiki	common sense/knowledge	408
識別	shikibetsu	discrimination, recognition	167

識

487

土 立 十
3b 54 12

KŌ, saiwa(i), shiawa(se), sachi – happiness, good fortune

幸運	kōun	good fortune, luck	214
行幸	gyōkō	visit/attendance by the emperor	49
不幸	fukō	unhappiness, misfortune	100

幸

488

報
3b 54 12

HŌ – news, report; remuneration **muku(iru)** – reward, requite

情報	jōhō	information	291
報道機関	hōdō kikan	news media, the press	120, 423, 373
天気予報	tenki yohō	weather forecast	73, 72, 370
報知	hōchi	information, news, intelligence	147

489

辞
5b/54 24 12

JI – word; resignation **ya(meru)** – quit, resign

辞書	jisho	dictionary	70
（お）世辞	(o)seji	compliment, flattery	163
式辞	shikiji	address, oration	422
辞職	jishoku	resignation	367

490

告
3d/24 22 2

KOKU, tsu(geru) – tell, announce, inform

報告	hōkoku	report	488
申告	shinkoku	report, declaration, (tax) return	332
告発	kokuhatsu	prosecution, indictment, accusation	101
告白	kokuhaku	confession, avowal, profession	75

491

洗
3a/21 22 16

SEN, ara(u) – wash

洗面	senmen	washing the face	318
洗面所	senmenjo	washroom, lavatory	318, 270
洗礼	senrei	baptism	462
（お）手洗い	(o)tearai	washroom, lavatory	89

492

宀 忩 儿
3m/33 51 16

SŌ, mado – window

同窓生	*dōsōsei*	schoolmate, alumnus	141, 36
車窓	*shasō*	car window	71
窓口	*madoguchi*	(ticket) window	87
窓際の席	*madogiwa no seki*	seat next to the window	460, 364

493

辶 王 尸
2q/19 46 40

CHI, oso(i) – late, tardy; slow **oku(reru)** – be late (for); be slow (clock) **oku(rasu)** – defer; put back (a clock)

遅配	*chihai*	delay in apportioning/delivery	416
遅着	*chichaku*	late arrival	239
乗り遅れる	*noriokureru*	be too late to catch, miss (a bus/train)	421

494

言 攵 艹
7a/67 49 32

KEI – admonish, warn

警察	*keisatsu*	police	461
警官	*keikan*	policeman	341
警告	*keikoku*	warning, admonition	490
警報	*keihō*	warning (signal), alarm	488

495

彳 阝 宀
3i/29 7 15

GYO, GO, on- – (honorific prefix)

制御	*seigyo*	control, governing, suppression	388
御飯	*gohan*	boiled rice; meal	185
御用の方	*goyō no kata*	customer, inquirer	106, 94
御所	*gosho*	imperial palace	270

496

加
力 口
2g/8 24

KA – add, append **kuwa(eru)** – join, take part (in) **kuwa(waru)** – increase; join in

加法	kahō	addition (in math)	262
加速度	kasokudo	acceleration	411, 200
加入	kanyū	joining	43
加工	kakō	processing	116

497

参
彡 大 厶
3j/31 34 17

SAN – three (in documents), go, come, visit **mai(ru)** – go, come, visit, visit a temple/shrine

参加	sanka	participation	496
参列	sanretsu	attendance, presence	456
参考書	sankōsho	reference book/work	235, 70
参議院	Sangiin	(Japanese) House of Councilors	323, 238

498

増
土 田 日
3b/22 58 42

ZŌ, ma(su) – increase, rise **fu(eru)** – increase, raise **fu(yasu)** – increase, rise

増加	zōka	increase, rise, growth	496
増産	zōsan	increase in production	321
増進	zōshin	increase, furtherance, improvement	391
水増し	mizumashi	water down, dilute, pad	19

499

富
宀 田 口
3m/33 58 24

FU, [FŪ] – wealth **tomi** – wealth; lottery ticket **to(mu)** – be/become rich

国富	kokufu	national wealth	33
富強	fukyō	wealth and power (of a nation)	148
富力	furyoku	wealth, resources	104
富山市	Toyama-shi	(city of) Toyama (Toyama-ken)	31, 279

500 | KYŪ, moto(meru) – seek, want, request, demand

2b 21 1

求

要求	yōkyū	demand	383
求職	kyūshoku	seeking employment, job hunting	367
求人	kyūjin	job offer, Help Wanted	1
探求	tankyū	research, investigation	427

501 | KYŪ, tama – ball, sphere

4f/46 21 1

球

野球	yakyū	baseball	157
球場	kyūjō	baseball stadium, ball park	122
地球	chikyū	the earth, globe	110
北半球	kita-hankyū	Northern Hemisphere	53, 59

502 | KEN – matter, affair, case

2a/3 47

件

事件	jiken	incident, affair, case	96
要件	yōken	important matter; condition, requisite	383
用件	yōken	(item of) business	106
物件	bukken	thing, article, physical object, a property	95

503 | BAN – evening, night

4c/42 24 15

晩

今晩	konban	this evening, tonight	42
毎晩	maiban	every evening	69
一晩	hitoban	a night, all night	2
晩年	bannen	latter part of one's life	37

504 言 亻 十
7a/67 15 12

KYO, yuru(su) – permit, allow

許可	kyoka	permission, approval, authorization	369
許容	kyoyō	permission, tolerance	473
特許	tokkyo	special permission; patent	172
特許法	tokkyo-hō	patent law	172, 262

---

505 言 心 力
7a/67 51 8

NIN, mito(meru) – perceive; recognize; approve of

認可	ninka	approval	369
認定	nintei	approval, acknowledgment	351
確認	kakunin	confirmation, certification	451
認識	ninshiki	cognition, recognition, perception	486

---

506 糸 尸 𠃌
6a/61 40 15

ZETSU, ta(eru) – die out, end **ta(tsu)** – cut off, interrupt; eradicate **ta(yasu)** – kill off, let die out

絶対	zettai	absolute	357
絶大	zetsudai	greatest, immense	24
絶望	zetsubō	despair	484
中絶	chūzetsu	termination; abortion	26

---

507 貝 大 一
7b/68 34 1

SAN – praise, agreement

賛成	sansei	agreement, approbation	311
不賛成	fusansei	disapproval, disagreement	100, 311
賛助	sanjo	support, backing	464
賛美	sanbi	praise, glorification	375

508	声尸｜ 3p/22 40 2	**SEI, [SHŌ], koe, [kowa-]** – voice

声明　　*seimei*　　declaration, statement, proclamation　　81
名声　　*meisei*　　fame, reputation　　57
音声学　*onseigaku*　phonetics　　192, 65
声色　　*kowairo*　　imitated/assumed voice　　142

509	貝弓儿 7b/68 28 16	**HI** – expenses, cost **tsui(yasu)** – spend **tsui(eru)** – be wasted

経費　　*keihi*　　expenses, cost　　433
費用　　*hiyō*　　expense, cost　　106
生活費　*seikatsuhi*　living expenses, cost of living; heating and lighting expenses　　36, 301
旅費　　*ryohi*　　traveling expenses　　151

510	貝欠冫 7b/68 49 5	**SHI** – resources, capital, funds

資本　　*shihon*　　capital　　23
資金　　*shikin*　　funds　　21
物資　　*busshi*　　goods, (raw) materials　　95
資格　　*shikaku*　　qualification, competence　　469

511	儿貝力 2o/16 68 8	**HIN, BIN, mazu(shii)** – poor

貧富　　*hinpu*　　poverty and wealth, the rich and poor　　499
貧困　　*hinkon*　　poor, meager, scanty　　439
貧相　　*hinsō*　　poor-looking, seedy　　266
貧民　　*hinmin*　　the poor　　276

512	又 丨
	2h/9 2

SHŪ, osa(meru) – obtain, collect **osa(maru)** – be obtained, end

収支	shūshi	income and expenditures	337
収入	shūnyū	income, receipts, revenue, earnings	43
収容	shūyō	admission, accommodation	473
回収	kaishū	recover, reclaim, collect, withdraw from circulation	256

513	日 勿
	4c/42 27

EKI – divination **I, yasa(shii)** – easy

易者	ekisha	fortune-teller	129
不易	fueki	immutability, unchangeableness	100
交易	kōeki	trade, commerce, barter	259
容易	yōi	easy, simple	473

514	田 厂 力
	5f/58 18 8

RYŪ, [RU], to(meru) – fasten down, hold, keep (in) **to(maru)** – stay, settle

留学	ryūgaku	study abroad	65
在留	zairyū	reside, stay	315
留守	rusu	absence from home	406
書留	kakitome	registered mail	70

515	艹 日 一
	3k/32 42 1

SEKI, [SHAKU], mukashi – antiquity, long ago

昔日	sekijitsu	old/former times	5
今昔	konjaku	past and present	42
昔々	mukashi-mukashi	Once upon a time ...	
昔話	mukashi-banashi	old tale, legend	76

516 — 散

攵 月 艹
4i/49 43 32

SAN – scatter, disperse **chi(rakasu)** – scatter, strew **chi(rakaru)** – lie scattered, be in disorder
chi(rasu) – (tr.) scatter **chi(ru)** – (intr.) scatter

解散	kaisan	breakup, dissolution, disbanding	401
散文	sanbun	prose	108
散歩	sanpo	walk, stroll	211

517 — 備

亻 月 艹
2a/3 43 32

BI, sona(eru) – furnish, provide (for) **sona(waru)** – possess

予備	yobi	preparatory, preliminary, in reserve, spare	370
予備知識	yobi chishiki	preliminary knowledge, background	370, 147, 486
守備	shubi	defense	406
備考	bikō	explanatory notes, remarks	235

518 — 込

辶 亻
2g/19 3

ko(mu) – be crowded, congested **ko(meru)** – include, count in; load (a gun); concentrate

払い込む	haraikomu	pay in	448
申し込み	mōshikomi	proposal, offer, application	332
見込み	mikomi	prospects, outlook	46
やり込める	yarikomeru	talk down, refute, corner	

519 — 横

木 日 艹
4a/41 42 32

Ō, yoko – side; horizontal direction

横道	yokomichi	side street; side issue, digression	120
横切る	yokogiru	cross, traverse	85
横顔	yokogao	profile	320
横目	yokome	side glance; amorous glance	88

520	广 土 亻
	3q/18 22 3

ZA – seat; theater; constellation **suwa(ru)** – sit down

座席	*zaseki*	seat	364
座談会	*zadankai*	round-table discussion, symposium	450, 125
口座	*kōza*	(savings) account	87
銀座	*Ginza*	(area of Tōkyō); busy shopping street/area	181

521	刂 ヨ 丨
	3d/24 39 2

KUN – (suffix for male personal names); ruler **kimi** – you (in masculine speech); ruler

田中君	*Tanaka-kun*	(Mr.) Tanaka	84, 26
君主	*kunshu*	monarch, sovereign	123
母君	*hahagimi*	mother (polite)	66
君が代	*Kimigayo*	(Japan's national anthem)	165

522	辶 弓 卄
	2q/19 28 32

SEN, era(bu) – choose, select

当選	*tōsen*	be elected	251
精選	*seisen*	careful selection	477
予選	*yosen*	preliminary match; primary election	370
選手	*senshu*	(sports) player	89

523	一 卄 夕
	0a 32 30

BU, ma(u) – dance, flutter about **mai** – dance

舞台	*butai*	the stage	229
仕舞	*shimai*	end, conclusion	188
舞い上がる	*maiagaru*	fly up, soar	29
（お）見舞い	*(o)mimai*	visit, inquiry (after someone's health)	46

524 ⺾ 目 夕 | 3k/32 55 30

MU, yume – dream

夢想	*musō*	dream, vision, fancy	267
悪夢	*akumu*	bad dream, nightmare	178
夢中	*muchū*	rapture; absorption, intentness; frantic	26
夢を見る	*yume o miru*	(have a) dream	46

525 辶 口 十 | 2q/19 24 12

I – be different; violation **chiga(u)** – be different; be mistaken **chiga(eru)** – alter; violate

相違	*sōi*	difference, disparity	266
違反	*ihan*	violation	340
違法	*ihō*	illegal	262
間違い	*machigai*	mistake, error; accident, mishap	35

526 冫 亻 一 | 2b/5 3 1

REI, tsume(tai) – cold **hi(yasu), sa(masu)** – chill, cool **hi(eru), sa(meru)** – become cold **hi(ya)** – cold water; cold saké **hi(yakasu)** – poke fun at, tease; browse

冷水	*reisui*	cold water	19
冷戦	*reisen*	cold war	328
冷静	*reisei*	calm, cool, dispassionate	479

527 ⺾ 夂 氵 | 3k/32 49 21

RAKU, o(chiru) – fall **o(tosu)** – drop, lose

転落	*tenraku*	a fall	212
部落	*buraku*	village, settlement	254
落語	*rakugo*	Japanese comic storytelling	48
落ち着いた	*ochitsuita*	calm, composed	239

528 消

氵 月 小
3a/21　43　35

SHŌ, ke(su) – extinguish; erase **ki(eru)** – go out, disappear

費消	hishō	spending; embezzlement	509
消費者	shōhisha	consumer	509, 129
消化	shōka	digestion	307
消しゴム	keshigomu	eraser	

529 退

辶 食
2q/19　77

TAI, shirizo(ku) – retreat **shirizo(keru)** – drive away, repel

退職	taishoku	retirement, resignation	367
退院	taiin	leave/be discharged from the hospital	238
退学	taigaku	leave/drop out of school	65
引退	intai	retire (from public life)	293

530 限

阝 食
2d/7　77

GEN, kagi(ru) – limit

制限	seigen	restriction, limitation	388
限度	gendo	a limit	200
期限	kigen	term, time limit, deadline	398
権限	kengen	authority, competence, jurisdiction	345

531 眠

目 尸 十
5c/55　40　12

MIN, nemu(ru) – sleep **nemu(i)** – tired, sleepy

不眠	fumin	sleeplessness, insomnia	100
安眠	anmin	a quiet/sound sleep	105
居眠り	inemuri	a doze, falling asleep in one's seat	275
眠り薬	nemurigusuri	sleeping drug/pills	353

532　日 日 小 4c/42 24 35	**KEI** – view, scene	
	景色　*keshiki*　scenery	142
	風景　*fūkei*　scenery	83
	景気　*keiki*　business conditions	72
	不景気　*fukeiki*　hard times, recession	100, 72

景

景　景　景

景　景　景

533　糸 日 土 6a/61 42 22	**SHO, [CHO]** – beginning **o** – cord, strap, thơng	
	緒戦　*shosen, chosen*　beginning of war	328
	緒論　*shoron, choron*　introduction	324
	由緒　*yuisho*　history; pedigree, lineage	356
	情緒　*jōcho, jōsho*　emotion, feeling	291

緒

緒　緒　緒

緒　緒　緒

534　戈 厶 亻 4n/52 17 3	**KI, iku** – how much/many; some	
	幾何学　*kikagaku*　geometry	80, 65
	幾日　*ikunichi*　how many days; what day of the month	5
	幾分　*ikubun*　some, a portion, more or less	32
	幾つ　*ikutsu*　how much/many/old	

幾

幾　幾　幾

幾　幾　幾

535　犭 阝 3g/27 7	**HAN** – crime **oka(su)** – commit (a crime); violate, defy	
	犯人　*hannin*　criminal, culprit	1
	犯行　*hankō*　crime	49
	現行犯で　*genkōhan de*　in the act, red-handed	326, 49
	共犯　*kyōhan*　complicity	284

犯

犯　犯　犯

犯　犯　犯

536
罒 冖 卜
5g/55 4 13

ZAI, tsumi – crime, sin, guilt

犯罪	*hanzai*	crime	535
罪人	*zainin, tsumibito*	criminal, sinner	1
罪悪感	*zaiakukan*	a sense/feelings of guilt	178, 312
有罪	*yūzai*	guilty	166

罪

537
扌 月 十
3c/23 43 12

HO, to(ru), to(raeru), tsuka(maeru) – catch, grasp **to(rawareru), tsuka(maru)** – be caught, hold on to

だ捕	*daho*	capture, seize	
分捕る	*bundoru*	capture, seize, plunder	32
捕り物	*torimono*	a capture, an arrest	95
生け捕り	*ikedori*	capturing alive	36

捕

538
宀 大 儿
3m/33 34 16

TOTSU, tsu(ku) – thrust, poke, strike

突然	*totsuzen*	suddenly	472
突破	*toppa*	break through, overcome	480
突入	*totsunyū*	rush in, storm	43
突き当たる	*tsukiataru*	run/bump into; reach the end	251

突

539
刂 土 厶
2f/16 22 17

TŌ – arrive, reach

到着	*tōchaku*	arrival	239
到来	*tōrai*	arrival, advent	50
到達	*tōtatsu*	reach, attain	397
殺到	*sattō*	rush, stampede	444

到

540	イ 土 儿 2a/3 22 16	**TŌ, tao(reru)** – fall over, collapse **tao(su)** – knock down, topple, defeat

倒産　　*tōsan*　　bankruptcy　　321
面倒　　*mendō*　　trouble, difficulty; taking care of, tending to　　318
共倒れ　*tomodaore*　mutual destruction, common ruin　　284
突き倒す　*tsukitaosu*　knock down　　538

倒　倒　倒

倒　倒　倒

541	言 口 儿 7a/67 24 16	**GO** – mistake, mis- **ayama(ru)** – err, make a mistake

誤解　　*gokai*　　misunderstanding　　401
誤報　　*gohō*　　erroneous report/information　　488
誤用　　*goyō*　　misuse　　106
読み誤る　*yomiayamaru*　misread　　77

誤　誤　誤

誤　誤　誤

542	一 丁 一 0a 14 1	**GO, taga(i)** – mutual, reciprocal, each other

相互　　*sōgo*　　mutual　　266
交互　　*kōgo*　　mutual; alternating　　259
互助　　*gojo*　　mutual aid　　464
互い違いに　*tagaichigai ni*　alternately　　525

互　互　互

互　互　互

543	イ 糸 丨 2a/3 61 2	**KEI, kaka(ru)** – have to do with **kakari** – person in charge

関係　　*kankei*　　relation, relationship, connection　　373
関係者　*kankeisha*　interested party, those concerned　　373, 129
係争　　*keisō*　　dispute, contention　　329
係長　　*kakarichō*　chief clerk　　60

係　係　係

係　係　係

544

心 貝 攵
4k/51 68 25

慣

KAN, na(reru) – get used to **na(rasu)** – accustom to; tame

習慣	*shūkan*	custom, practice	237
慣習	*kanshū*	custom, practice	237
慣例	*kanrei*	custom, convention	457
見慣れる	*minareru*	get used to seeing	46

慣 慣 慣

慣 慣 慣

545

火 口 土
4d/44 24 22

煙

EN, kemuri – smoke **kemu(ru)** – smoke, smolder **kemu(i)** – smoky

煙突	*entotsu*	chimney	538
発煙	*hatsuen*	emitting smoke, fuming	101
黒煙	*kokuen*	black smoke	143
煙たがる	*kemutagaru*	suffer from smoke (in a room); want to avoid	

煙 煙 煙

煙 煙 煙

546

口 鳥
3d/24 80

鳴

MEI, na(ku) – (animals) cry, sing, howl **na(ru)** – (intr.) sound, ring **na(rasu)** – (tr.) sound, ring

共鳴	*kyōmei*	resonance; sympathy	284
鳴動	*meidō*	rumble	156
鳴き声	*nakigoe*	cry, call, chirping (of animals)	508
海鳴り	*uminari*	rumbling/noise of the sea	109

鳴 鳴 鳴

鳴 鳴 鳴

547

氵 小 子
3a/21 35 6

浮

FU, u(kabu) – float, rise to the surface, appear **u(kaberu)** – set afloat; show **u(ku)** – float, rise to the surface **u(kareru)** – feel buoyant, be in high spirits

思い浮ぶ	*omoiukabu*	come to mind, occur to	103
浮かぬ顔	*ukanu kao*	dejected look	320
浮世絵	*ukiyoe*	Japanese woodblock print	163, 348

浮 浮 浮

浮 浮 浮

548	亻 大 ㇒ 2a/3 34 15	**KŌ** – season; weather **sōrō** – (classical verb suffix)	
候		時候 *jikō* season, time of year; weather	34
		天候 *tenkō* weather	73
		気候 *kikō* climate	72
		居候 *isōrō* hanger-on, parasite	275

549	阝 夂 十 2d/7 49 12	**KŌ, o(riru)** – go down, descend, get off (a bus) **o(rosu)** – let off (a passenger), dismiss **fu(ru)** – fall	
降		降雨 *kōu* rain(fall) (rain/snow)	27
		降下 *kōka* descent, fall, landing	28
		以降 *ikō* since, from ... on	86
		飛び降りる *tobioriru* jump down (from)	424

550	雪 ヨ 8d/74 39	**SETSU, yuki** – snow	
雪		残雪 *zansetsu* lingering snow	471
		初雪 *hatsuyuki* first snow of the year/winter	485
		雪空 *yukizora* snowy sky	117
		雪景色 *yukigeshiki* snowy landscape	532, 142

551	口 火 儿 3d/24 44 16	**TŌ, TO, nobo(ru)** – climb	
登		登場 *tōjō* stage entrance; appearance	122
		登記 *tōki* registration	359
		登用 *tōyō* appointment; promotion	106
		登山 *tozan* mountain climbing	31

552

辶 米
2q/19 62

MEI, mayo(u) – be perplexed, vacillate; get lost; go astray

迷路	*meiro*	maze, labyrinth	269
迷信	*meishin*	superstition	271
気迷い	*kimayoi*	hesitation, wavering	72
迷子	*maigo*	lost child	63

553

彳 厂 又
3i/29 18 9

HI – he, that **kare** – he *[kano]* – that

彼ら	*karera*	they	
彼女	*kanojo*	she; girlfriend, lover	62

554

扌 日 丨
3c/23 42 2

Ō, o(su) – push **o(saeru)** – restrain, hold in check, suppress

押収	*ōshū*	confiscation	512
押し入れ	*oshiire*	closet, wall-cupboard	43
後押し	*atooshi*	push, support, back	39
押し付ける	*oshitsukeru*	press against; force (upon)	283

555

戈 土 卜
4n/52 22 13

ETSU, ko(su) – cross, go over, exceed **ko(eru)** – cross, go over; clear, surmount

越冬	*ettō*	pass the winter	221
引っ越す	*hikkosu*	move, change residences	293
借り越す	*karikosu*	overdraw	244
勝ち越し	*kachikoshi*	a net win, being ahead	412

556

遊 2q/19 48 15

YŪ, [YU], aso(bu) – play, enjoy oneself, be idle

遊歩道	yūhodō	promenade, mall, boardwalk	211, 120
遊説	yūzei	speaking tour, political campaigning	374
外遊	gaiyū	foreign travel/trip	58
遊び相手	asobiaite	playmate	266, 89

557

更 0a 42 14

KŌ, sara – anew, again, furthermore **fu(kasu)** – stay up till late (at night) **fu(keru)** – grow late

変更	henkō	alteration, change, modification	308
更新	kōshin	renew, renovate, update	135
更生	kōsei	rebirth, rehabilitation	36
今更	imasara	now, at this late date	42

558

構 4a/41 32 22

KŌ, kama(eru) – build, set up, assume a posture/position **kama(u)** – mind, care about, meddle in, look after

機構	kikō	mechanism, structure, organization	423
構成	kōsei	composition, makeup	311
構想	kōsō	conception, plan	267
心構え	kokorogamae	mental attitude, readiness	102

559

打 3c/23 14

DA, u(tsu) – hit, strike

打開	dakai	a break, development, new turn	203
不意打ち	fuiuchi	surprise attack	100, 114
打ち合わせ	uchiawase	previous arrangement	272
打ち消し	uchikeshi	denial; negation	528

560 投   扌 冂 又   3c/23   20   9

TŌ, na(geru) – throw

投下	*tōka*	throw down, drop; invest	28
投書	*tōsho*	letter to the editor, contribution	70
投資	*tōshi*	investment	510
投機	*tōki*	speculation	423

561 断   米 斤 丨   6b/62   50   2

DAN – decision, judgment ***kotowa(ru)*** – decline, refuse; give warning; prohibit ***ta(tsu)*** – cut off

決断	*ketsudan*	(prompt) decision, resolution	352
断行	*dankō*	carry out (resolutely)	49
断念	*dannen*	abandonment, giving up	446
横断歩道	*ōdan hodō*	pedestrian crossing	519, 211, 120

562 判   刂 十 一   2f/16   12   1

HAN – stamp, seal ***BAN*** – (paper) size

判断（力）	*handan(ryoku)*	judgment	561, 104
判決	*hanketsu*	a decision, ruling	352
判事	*hanji*	a judge	96
公判	*kōhan*	(public) trial	113

563 優   亻 月 心   2a/3   43   51

YŪ – superior; gentle; actor ***sugu(reru)*** – excel ***yasa(shii)*** – gentle, tender, kindhearted

優越	*yūetsu*	superiority, supremacy	555
優勝	*yūshō*	victory, championship	412
優先	*yūsen*	priority	41
女優	*joyū*	actress	62

564	悲 二 ⼘ 4k/51　4　13	**HI, kana(shii)** – sad **kana(shimu)** – be sad, lament, regret	
		悲報　　*hihō*　　sad news	488
		悲運　　*hiun*　　misfortune, hard luck	214
		悲鳴　　*himei*　　shriek, scream	546
		悲観　　*hikan*　　pessimism	452

565	扌 日 ⼘ 3c/23　42　13	**SHI** – finger; point to, direct **yubi** – finger **sa(su)** – point to	
		指南　　*shinan*　　instruction, guidance	54
		指名　　*shimei*　　nomination, designation	57
		指定席　　*shiteiseki*　　reserved seat	351, 364
		人さし指　　*hitosashiyubi*　　index finger, forefinger	1

566	亻 日 十 2a/3　24　12	**I, era(i)** – great, eminent, extraordinary, excellent	
		偉大　　*idai*　　great, mighty, grand	24
		偉人　　*ijin*　　great man	1
		偉才　　*isai*　　man of extraordinary talent	435
		偉業　　*igyō*　　great achievement	169

567	辶 厂 阝 2q/19　18　7	**GEI, muka(eru)** – go to meet, receive, invite, send for	
		送迎　　*sōgei*　　welcome and sendoff	215
		迎合　　*geigō*　　flattery	272
		迎え入れる　　*mukaeireru*　　usher in, welcome	43
		出迎え　　*demukae*　　meeting (someone) on arrival, reception	44

568	亻 朩 一 2a/3　41　1	**YO, ama(ru)** – be left over, in excess **ama(su)** – leave over	
		二十余年　*nijūyonen*　more than 20 years	3, 12, 37
		余命　*yomei*　the rest of one's life	445
		余計　*yokei*　too much, unwanted, uncalled-for	190
		余地　*yochi*　room, margin	110

余　余　余

569	阝 朩 亻 2d/7　41　3	**JO, [JI], nozo(ku)** – get rid of, exclude	
		解除　*kaijo*　cancellation	401
		除名　*jomei*　remove (someone's) name, expel	57
		除外　*jogai*　except, exclude	58
		取り除く　*torinozoku*　remove, rid	250

除　除　除

570	辶 朩 亻 2q/19　41　3	**TO** – way, road	
		途中　*tochū*　on the way, midway	26
		前途　*zento*　one's future, prospects	38
		途絶える　*todaeru*　come to a stop	506
		（開発）途上国　*(kaihatsu) tojōkoku*　developing country	203, 101, 29, 33

途　途　途

571	艹 口 亻 3k/32　24　3	**KA, kutsu** – shoe	
		靴屋　*kutsuya*　shoe store	132
		運動靴　*undōgutsu*　athletic shoes, sneakers	214, 156
		靴下　*kutsushita*　socks, stockings	28
		靴一足　*kutsu issoku*　one pair of shoes	2, 90

靴　靴　靴

572	宀 ヨ ⺅ 3m/33 39 5	**SHIN, ne(ru)** – go to bed, sleep **ne(kasu)** – put to bed	
		寝室　*shinshitsu*　bedroom	131
		寝台　*shindai*　bed	229
		昼寝　*hirune*　(daytime) nap, siesta	226
		寝苦しい　*negurushii*　unable to sleep well	432

寝　寝　寝

寝　寝　寝

573	⺮ 目 木 6f/66 55 41	**hako** – box	
		小箱　*kobako*　small box/case	25
		本箱　*honbako*　bookcase	23
		重箱　*jūbako*　nested boxes	153
		箱入り　*hakoiri*　boxed, in cases; precious, sheltered	43

箱　箱　箱

箱　箱　箱

574	皿 夂 ⺅ 5h/59 49 5	**TŌ, nusu(mu)** – steal	
		強盗　*gōtō*　burglar, robber	148
		盗難　*tōnan*　theft	438
		盗作　*tōsaku*　plagiarism	198
		盗用　*tōyō*　embezzlement; fraudulent use; plagiarism	106

盗　盗　盗

盗　盗　盗

575	广 王 廴 3q/18 46 19	**TEI, niwa** – garden	
		家庭　*katei*　home, family	130
		庭球　*teikyū*　tennis	501
		校庭　*kōtei*　schoolyard, school grounds	68
		庭園　*teien*　garden	396

庭　庭　庭

庭　庭　庭

576 欠 火 口
4j/49 44 24

YOKU – covetousness, desire ***hos(suru), ho(shii)*** – desire, want

食欲	*shokuyoku*	appetite	79
性欲	*seiyoku*	sexual desire, sex drive	257
欲望	*yokubō*	desire, appetite, craving	484
欲求不満	*yokkyū fuman*	frustration	500, 100, 288

欲

577 夂 冂
4i/49 20

SHO – deal with, treat; sentence, condemn; behave, act

処分	*shobun*	disposal, disposition; punishment	32
処置	*shochi*	disposition, measures, steps	387
対処	*taisho*	cope with, tackle	357
処女	*shojo*	virgin	62

処

578 喜 口 儿
3p/22 24 16

KI, yoroko(bu) – be glad

喜色満面	*kishoku-manmen*	beaming face, all smiles	142, 288, 318
悲喜	*hiki*	joy and sorrow	564
大喜び	*ōyorokobi*	great joy	24
喜ばしい	*yorokobashii*	joyful, pleasant, gratifying	

喜

579 彡 十 又
3j/31 12 9

HATSU, kami – hair (on the head)

散髪	*sanpatsu*	haircut, hairdressing	516
洗髪	*senpatsu*	hair washing, a shampoo	491
間一髪	*kan'ippatsu*	a hairbreadth (escape)	35, 2
白髪	*hakuhatsu, shiraga*	white/gray hair	75

髪

580

木 一 丨
4a/41 14 2

HAI – cup; (counter for cupfuls) **sakazuki** – winecup (for saké)

一杯	*ippai*	a glass (of); a drink; full	2
精一杯	*seiippai*	with all one's might, as best as one can	477, 2
銀杯	*ginpai*	silver cup	181
苦杯	*kuhai*	bitter cup, ordeal, defeat	432

581

辶 尸 冂
2q/19 40 20

TSUI, o(u) – drive away, pursue

追放	*tsuihō*	banishment, purge	415
追求	*tsuikyū*	pursue, follow up	500
追加	*tsuika*	addition, supplement	496
追い越す	*oikosu*	overtake, pass	555

582

言 方
7a/67 48

HŌ, tazu(neru), otozu(reru) – visit

訪問	*hōmon*	visit	127
来訪	*raihō*	visit	50
訪客	*hōkyaku*	visitor, guest	468
探訪	*tanbō*	inquiries, inquiring into	427

583

氵 丶
3a/21 2

EI, oyo(gu) – swim

水泳	*suiei*	swimming	19
泳法	*eihō*	swimming style/stroke	262
遠泳	*en'ei*	long-distance swim	395
平泳ぎ	*hiraoyogi*	the breaststroke	289

584 刻

2f/16 11 17

KOKU – time; carve **kiza(mu)** – cut fine, chop up, carve, engrave

時刻	jikoku	time; hour	34
夕刻	yūkoku	evening	97
一刻	ikkoku	moment; stubborn	2
深刻	shinkoku	grave, serious	428

585 笑

6f/66 34 2

SHŌ, wara(u) – laugh **e(mu)** – smile

苦笑／苦笑い	kushō / nigawarai	wry smile, forced laugh	432
談笑	danshō	friendly talk, chat	450
大笑い	ōwarai	loud laughter, hearty laugh	24
笑顔	egao	smiling face	320

586 戻

4m/40 34

REI – rebel; perverse **modo(ru)** – go/come back, return **modo(su)** – give/send back, return, restore, throw up; vomit

取り戻す	torimodosu	take back, regain, recoup	250
払い戻す	haraimodosu	pay back, refund	448
立ち戻る	tachimodoru	return to	111
戻り道	modorimichi	the way back	120

587 息

4k/51 55 2

SOKU – son; breath **iki** – breath

休息	kyūsoku	a rest, breather	45
消息	shōsoku	news, information	528
息切れ	ikigire	shortness of breath	85
息子	musuko	son	63

588

口 丆 丨
3d/24　14　2

HI – no, negative **ina** – no, nay

否定	hitei	denial, negation	351
否認	hinin	denial, repudiation, disavow	505
否決	hiketsu	rejection, voting down	352
賛否	sanpi	approval or disapproval, yes or no	507

否

否 否 否

否 否 否

589

口 十 几
3d/24　12　16

KO, yo(bu) – call, send for, invite, name

点呼	tenko	roll call	273
呼び声	yobigoe	a call, cry, shout	508
呼び出す	yobidasu	call out/up/forth, summon	44
呼び戻す	yobimodosu	call back, recall	586

呼

呼 呼 呼

呼 呼 呼

590

口 攵
3d/24　49

SUI, fu(ku) – blow

吹鳴	suimei	blowing (of a whistle)	546
吹雪	fubuki	snowstorm	550
吹き出し	fukidashi	blowoff, bleeder (valve); speech balloon	44
吹き飛ばす	fukitobasu	be blown away	424

吹

吹 吹 吹

吹 吹 吹

591

口 力 丨
3d/24　8　2

KYŪ, su(u) – suck in, inhale, smoke

呼吸	kokyū	breathing	589
吸入	kyūnyū	inhale	43
吸引	kyūin	absorb (by suction)	293
吸収	kyūshū	absorb	512

吸

吸 吸 吸

吸 吸 吸

592 月 卜 一 4b/43 13 1

HAI, se – back, height **sei** – height, stature **somu(ku)** – act contrary (to) **somu(keru)** – avert, turn away

背景	haikei	background	532
背信	haishin	breach of faith, betrayal, infidelity	271
背中	senaka	the back	26
背広	sebiro	business suit	241

593 月 日 夊 4b/43 42 49

FUKU, hara – belly, heart, mind

切腹	seppuku	disembowelment, harakiri	85
立腹	rippuku	anger, offense	111
空腹	kūfuku	empty belly, hunger	117
脇腹	wakibara	one's side, flank; illeigitmate child	

594 一 弓 勹 0a 28 15

HŌ, tsutsu(mu) – wrap up

包容力	hōyōryoku	capacity; tolerance, broad-mindedness	473, 104
小包	kozutsumi	parcel	25
紙包み	kamizutsumi	parcel wrapped in paper	138
包み紙	tsutsumigami	wrapping paper, wrapper	138

595 疒 月 一 5i/60 43 1

TSŪ – pain; penetrating **ita(mu)** – feel painful, hurt **ita(meru)** – hurt, cause pain **ita(i)** – painful

苦痛	kutsū	pain	432
頭痛	zutsū	headache	319
痛飲	tsūin	drink heavily, carouse	184
痛手	itade	severe wound; hard blow	89

596

疒 广 厂 又
5i/60 18 9

HI, tsuka(reru) – get tired, become exhausted

疲労	*hirō*	fatigue, weariness	299
気疲れ	*kizukare*	mental fatigue/exhaustion	72
疲れ果てる	*tsukarehateru*	be completely exhausted	405
お疲れ様	*otsukaresama*	Thank you (for your tiring work).	376

疲　疲　疲

疲　疲　疲

597

宀 大 卩
3m/33 34 24

KI – depend on; give **yo(ru)** – approach, draw near, meet, drop in **yo(seru)** – bring near, push aside, gather together, send

寄付	*kifu*	contribution, donation	283
寄生	*kisei*	parasitism	36
立ち寄る	*tachiyoru*	drop in, stop (at)	111

寄　寄　寄

寄　寄　寄

598

忄 亠 丨
4k/51 11 2

BŌ, isoga(shii) – busy, be very occupied

多忙	*tabō*	busy, hectic	154
御多忙中	*gotabōchū*	(while you are so busy)	495, 154, 26
忙殺される	*bōsatsu sareru*	be busily occupied	444

忙　忙　忙

忙　忙　忙

599

亠 心 丨
2j/11 51 2

BŌ, wasu(reru) – forget

備忘	*bibō*	reminder	517
忘年会	*bōnenkai*	year-end party	37, 125
忘れ物	*wasuremono*	article left behind	95
度忘れ	*dowasure*	forget for the moment	200

忘　忘　忘

忘　忘　忘

600

礻 畐 口
4e/45 58 24

FUKU – fortune, blessing, wealth, welfare

幸福	*kōfuku*	happiness	487
福音	*fukuin*	the Gospel; good news	192
福引き	*fukubiki*	lottery, raffle	293
七福神	*Shichifukujin*	the Seven Gods of Good Fortune	9, 333

601

扌 斤
3c/23 50

SETSU – break; fold; turn (left/right) **o(ru)** – (tr.) fold; break; bend **o(reru)** – (intr.) break; be folded; yield, compromise; turn (left/right) **ori** – occasion, opportunity

右折	*usetsu*	right turn	56
曲折	*kyokusetsu*	twists and turns, complications	358
折り紙	*origami*	paper folding; paper for origami	138

602

艹 日 大
3k/32 42 34

BO, ku(reru) – grow dark, come to an end **ku(rasu)** – live

（お）歳暮	*(o)seibo*	end of the year; year-end gift	403
野暮	*yabo*	uncouth, rustic, boorish	157
夕暮れ	*yūgure*	evening, twilight	97
一人暮らし	*hitorigurashi*	living alone	2, 1

603

頁 一
9a/76 14

CHŌ, itadaki – summit, top **itada(ku)** – be capped with, receive

頂上	*chōjō*	summit, peak, top; climax	29
山頂	*sanchō*	summit, mountain top	31
頂点	*chōten*	zenith, peak, climax	273
絶頂	*zetchō*	peak, height, climax	506

---

604 | 扌 土 卜
3c/23 22 13

ka(karu) – hang; cost, take **ka(keru)** – hang up, put on top of; spend; multiply **kakari** – expenses; tax; relation, connection

出掛ける	*dekakeru*	go out, set out	44
心掛け	*kokorogake*	intention; attitude; attention	102
大掛り	*ōgakari*	large-scale	24

掛

---

605 | 犭 田 艹
3g/27 58 32

BYŌ, neko – cat

愛猫	*aibyō*	pet/favorite cat	309
猫背	*nekoze*	round shoulders, hunchback	592
招き猫	*manekineko*	beckoning (porcelain) cat	399
猫に小判	*Neko ni koban.*	To cast pearls before swine.	25, 562

猫

---

606 | 亻 丨
2a/3 2

JI, ni(ru) – be similar (to), be like, resemble

類似	*ruiji*	resemblance, similarity	296
似顔	*nigao*	likeness, portrait	320
空似	*sorani*	accidental resemblance	117
似合う	*niau*	be becoming, suit, go well (with)	272

似

---

607 | 頁 木 口
9a/76 41 24

RAI, tano(mu) – ask for, request, entrust (to) **tano(moshii)** – reliable, dependable, promising **tayo(ru)** – rely, depend (on)

信頼	*shinrai*	reliance, trust, confidence	271
人頼み	*hitodanomi*	relying on others	1
頼み込む	*tanomikomu*	earnestly request	518

頼

608

士 天 仁
2m/13 34 15

GI, utaga(u) – doubt, distrust, be suspicious of

疑問	*gimon*	question, doubt, problem	127
疑念	*ginen*	doubt, suspicion, misgivings	446
容疑者	*yōgisha*	a suspect	473, 129
疑わしい	*utagawashii*	doubtful, suspicious	

609

辶 冫 儿
2q/19 5 16

TŌ, ni(geru) – run away, escape, flee **noga(reru)** – escape **ni(gasu), noga(su)** – let go, set free,

逃走	*tōsō*	escape, flight	⌐let escape　210
逃亡	*tōbō*	escape, flight, desertion	483
逃げ出す	*nigedasu*	break into a run, run off/away	44
見逃す	*minogasu*	overlook	46

610

力 女 又
2g/8 25 9

DO, tsuto(meru) – exert oneself, make efforts, strive

努力	*doryoku*	effort, endeavor	104
努力家	*doryokuka*	hard worker	104, 130
努めて	*tsutomete*	as much as one can, diligently	

611

心 女 又
4k/51 25 9

DO, oko(ru), ika(ru) – become angry

怒気	*doki*	(fit of) anger	72
怒号	*dogō*	angry roar	314
怒り心頭に発する	*ikari shintō ni hassuru*	fly into a rage, explode in anger,	102, 319, 101
喜怒	*kido*	joy and anger, emotion	⌐make an angry outburst　578

612

心 工 冂
4k/51 38 20

KYŌ, oso(reru) – fear, be afraid of **oso(roshii)** – terrible, frightful, awful

恐妻家	kyōsaika	henpecked husband	482, 130
恐れ入る	osoreiru	be sorry to trouble, beg pardon	43
空恐ろしい	soraosoroshii	have a vague fear	117
恐らく	osoraku	probably, perhaps, maybe	

恐

613

亻 日 厶
2a/3 42 17

GŪ – chance, accidental; (married) couple; even number; doll

偶然	gūzen	chance, accident	472
偶発	gūhatsu	chance occurrence	101
配偶者	haigūsha	spouse	416, 129
偶数	gūsū	even number	295

偶

614

耳 心
6e/65 51

CHI, haji – shame, disgrace **ha(jiru)** – feel shame **ha(jirau)** – be shy **ha(zukashii)** – shy, ashamed

恥部	chibu	the private parts	254
恥じ入る	hajiiru	feel ashamed	43
生き恥	ikihaji	living in dishonor, shame	36
恥知らず	hajishirazu	shameless person	147

恥

615

扌 十 又
3c/23 12 9

BATSU, nu(ku) – pull out; remove; leave out; outdistance, surpass **nu(keru)** – come/fall out; be omitted; be gone; escape **nu(karu)** – make a blunder **nu(kasu)** – omit, skip over

選抜	senbatsu	selection, picking out	522
抜き出す	nukidasu	select, extract, pull out	44
気抜け	kinuke	lackadaisical; dispirited	72

抜

616	女 食 3e/25 77

musume – daughter, girl

小娘	komusume	(early-teenage) girl	25
娘心	musumegokoro	girlish mind/innocence	102
一人娘	hitori musume	an only daughter	2, 1
箱入り娘	hakoiri musume	girl who has led a sheltered life	573, 43

娘　娘　娘

娘　娘　娘

617	心 巾 十 4k/51 26 12

FU – fear **kowa(i)** – frightening, scary

恐怖	kyōfu	fear, terror	612
恐怖政治	kyōfu seiji	reign of terror	612, 404, 407
怖がる	kowagaru	fear, be afraid	

怖　怖　怖

怖　怖　怖

How to Use the Lookup Indexes

Each of the 617 kanji in the main part of this workbook can be looked up via the two indexes at the end of the book: by its reading or by its radical. The number to the right of each kanji entry in the indexes is the kanji's reference number telling where it will be found in the main part of this book.

Index by Readings

The alphabetically arranged Index by Readings is the easier to use when you know one of the readings of the desired kanji. Look up the kanji by its *kun* reading, if you know it. Otherwise you might have to scan through a long list of kanji having the same *on* reading.

Kanji with the same *on* reading are divided into groups each having the same pronunciation-indicating component, which is usually on the right side of the kanji. Example: *SEI* 青 情 晴 精. At the end of each group are kanji that contain this component and thus could also be looked for in this group, but which have a different reading. These kanji are listed in parentheses, with their actual reading given where their reference number would be.

Index by Radicals

If you do not know any reading of the kanji you are trying to find, try the Index by Radicals, which arranges the characters according to the 79-radical system of *The Kanji Dictionary* by Spahn/Hadamitzky. This system is made up of two parts: a table of radicals (page 288), and rules for determining the radical of a kanji (inside back cover).

The 79 radicals are arranged in increasing order of stroke-count, within the same stroke-count by their usual position within a kanji (left, right, top, bottom, enclosure, elsewhere), and within the same position by how frequently they occur (most common first).

The rules for determining a kanji's radical are a step-by-step checklist to decide which of two or more radical-candidate components of a kanji is actually its radical. For example, if both the left part and the right part of a kanji are listed in the radical table, the left part is its radical, according to the rule "left before right."

Having determined the radical, you look up the kanji in the Index by Radicals, in which the radicals are arranged in the same order as in the radical table. Under each radical, the characters are listed in increasing order of stroke count.

Index by Radicals

– 0a –
- 1 | 一 2
- 2 | 二 3 · 入 43 · 七 9 · 九 11
- 3 | 三 4 · 川 30 · 工 116 · 万 16 · 夕 97 · 大 24 · 与 429 · 才 435
- 4 | 不 100 · 元 115 · 予 370 · 互 542 · 太 466 · 天 73 · 内 253 · 五 7 · 夫 335 · 中 26
- 5 | 以 86 · 北 53 · 包 594 · 必 420 · 左 55 · 出 44 · 民 276 · 半 59 · 本 23 · 末 330 · 未 331 · 失 334 · 生 36 · 由 356 · 母 66 · 世 163 · 申 332
- 6 | 多 154 · 死 98 · 気 72 · 両 287 · 年 37 · 西 52 · 毎 69 · 曲 358
- 7 | 良 339 · 身 249 · 来 50 · 束 410 · 更 557 · 長 60
- 8 | 非 409 · 表 317 · 画 191 · 果 405 · 東 51 · 事 96
- 9 | 飛 424 · 発 101 · 重 153 · 乗 421
- 10 | 残 471
- 11 | 野 157
- 13 | 業 169
- 15 | 舞 523

– 2a – 亻
- 0 | 人 1
- 2 | 化 307 · 今 42
- 3 | 仕 188 · 代 165 · 他 260 · 付 283
- 4 | 休 45 · 件 502 · 任 344 · 伝 390 · 全 255 · 合 272 · 会 125 · 肉 152
- 5 | 位 261 · 体 91 · 作 198 · 似 606 · 住 124 · 何 80
- 6 | 余 187 · 使 457 · 例 285 · 供 446 · 念 445 · 命 271
- 7 | 信 343 · 便 543 · 係 540
- 8 | 倒 548 · 候 244 · 借 386 · 値 613
- 9 | 偶 455 · 側 517
- 10 | 備 566
- 11 | 働 298
- 15 | 優 563

– 2b – 冫
- 4 | 次 366
- 5 | 状 465 · 冷 526 · 求 500

– 2c – 子
- 0 | 子 63
- 3 | 存 316

– 2d – 阝
- 4 | 阪 394
- 6 | 限 530
- 7 | 降 549 · 院 238 · 除 569
- 8 | 険 425 · 都 282 · 部 254
- 9 | 陽 467
- 11 | 際 460

– 2f – 刂
- 2 | 切 85
- 4 | 列 456
- 5 | 判 562 · 別 167
- 6 | 制 388 · 到 539 · 刻 584
- 8 | 帰 182
- 10 | 割 419

– 2g – 力
- 0 | 力 104
- 3 | 加 496 · 助 464
- 5 | 努 610
- 9 | 動 156
- 10 | 勤 440

– 2h – 又
- 2 | 収 512 · 友 78
- 6 | 受 310

– 2i – 冖
- 3 | 写 234

– 2j – 亠
- 1 | 亡 483 · 六 8 · 文 108 · 市 279 · 交 259
- 6 | 忘 599 · 対 357 · 夜 227 · 京 140 · 育 303
- 7 | 変 308 · 高 74
- 9 | 商 378

– 2k – 十
- 0 | 十 12
- 1 | 千 15 · 支 337 · 午 40
- 3 | 古 134 · 平 289 · 考 235 · 老 430
- 6 | 直 385
- 7 | 南 54
- 8 | 真 209

– 2m – 卜
- 1 | 上 29 · 下 28
- 2 | 止 228
- 3 | 外 58 · 正 168
- 7 | 点 273
- 12 | 疑 608

– 2n – 勹
- 4 | 色 142 · 争 329 · 危 426
- 7 | 負 413 · 急 177
- 8 | 勉 242

– 2o – 丷
- 0 | 八 10
- 2 | 分 32 · 公 113 · 父 67 · 弟 204
- 7 | 首 268 · 前 38 · 美 375
- 8 | 差 476
- 9 | 貧 511 · 着 239

– 2p – 厂
- 2 | 反 340
- 8 | 原 264

– 2q – 辶
- 2 | 込 518
- 4 | 近 216 · 迎 567 · 返 393
- 6 | 迷 552 · 建 245 · 退 529 · 追 581 · 逃 609 · 送 215
- 7 | 連 392 · 速 411 · 途 570 · 通 121 · 進 391 · 遊 556 · 週 99
- 9 | 達 397 · 運 214 · 道 120 · 遅 493 · 過 379
- 10 | 遠 395 · 違 525
- 11 | 適 380
- 12 | 選 522

– 2r – 冂
- 2 | 円 13
- 3 | 用 106
- 4 | 同 141

– 2s – 几
- 7 | 風 83 · 段 355

– 2t – 匚
- 5 | 医 149

– 3a – 氵
- 0 | 水 19
- 4 | 決 352
- 5 | 泳 583 · 注 196 · 法 262 · 治 407
- 6 | 浮 547 · 洗 491 · 活 301 · 洋 175 · 海 109
- 7 | 酒 417 · 流 304 · 消 528
- 8 | 深 428 · 済 434
- 9 | 港 481 · 満 288 · 渡 363
- 10 | 漢 236
- 11 | 演 347

– 3b – 土
- 0 | 土 22
- 2 | 去 208
- 3 | 地 110 · 先 41
- 4 | 在 315 · 走 210
- 5 | 赤 144 · 幸 487 · 起 199
- 7 | 場 122
- 9 | 報 488
- 11 | 増 498

– 3c – 扌
- 0 | 手 89
- 2 | 払 448 · 打 559
- 4 | 折 601 · 抜 615 · 投 560
- 5 | 押 554 · 招 399
- 6 | 持 217 · 指 565
- 7 | 捕 537
- 8 | 掛 604 · 探 427

– 3d – 口

0	口	87
2	兄	205
	号	314
	台	229
	可	369
	右	56
3	吸	591
	向	286
	名	57
4	吹	590
	告	490
	否	588
	君	521
5	味	179
	呼	589
	知	147
6	品	155
7	員	128
9	登	551
11	鳴	546

– 3e – 女

0	女	62
2	好	258
5	妹	207
	姉	206
	始	230
	妻	482
6	要	383
7	娘	616
8	婚	441
	婦	336

– 3f – 巾

7	師	377

– 3g – 犭

0	犬	170
2	犯	535
8	猫	605

– 3h – 弓

1	引	293
8	強	148

– 3i – 彳

3	行	49
4	役	361
5	彼	553
6	待	218
	後	39
7	徒	389
8	術	281
	得	360
9	御	495

– 3j – 彡

4	形	371
5	参	497
11	髪	579

– 3k – 艹

3	共	284
4	花	164
5	英	194
	若	431
	苦	432
	昔	515
6	草	305
	茶	162
9	落	527
	葉	306
10	夢	524
	靴	571
11	暮	602
13	薬	353

– 3m – 宀

2	字	107
3	安	105
	守	406
	宅	277
4	究	246
	完	458
5	実	290
	官	341
	定	351
	突	538
	空	117
6	客	468
	室	131
7	家	130
	害	418
	容	473
8	宿	278
	窓	492
	寄	597
9	寒	400
10	富	499
	寝	572
11	察	461

– 3n – ⺌

0	小	25
1	少	119
3	光	265
	当	251
4	学	65
	労	299
5	歩	211
6	単	327
8	常	408
	堂	231
9	覚	453

– 3o – 山

0	山	31

– 3p – 士

4	売	158
	声	508
9	喜	578

– 3q – 广

2	広	241
5	店	133
6	度	200
	庭	575
	座	520
	席	364

– 3r – 尸

4	局	274
5	居	275
6	屋	132

– 3s – 囗

2	四	6
3	回	256
	因	437
4	困	439
	図	189
5	国	33
6	面	318
10	園	396

– 4a – 木

0	木	20
4	杯	580
5	相	266
6	格	469
	校	68
	殺	444
9	楽	197
10	構	558
	様	376
11	横	519
	権	345
12	機	423

– 4b – 月

0	月	17
2	有	166
4	服	240
	青	145
5	背	592
6	能	368
8	勝	412
	期	398
	朝	225
9	腹	593
10	静	479

– 4c – 日

0	日	5
1	白	75
2	早	161
	百	14
4	明	81
	易	513
	的	146
	者	129
5	映	193
	昨	354
	春	222
	皆	449
	昼	226
6	時	34
	書	70
7	習	237
8	晴	478
	晩	503
	景	532
	最	313
9	暗	350
14	曜	82

– 4d – 火

0	火	18
7	黒	143
8	然	472
9	煙	545
11	熱	470

– 4e – 礻

0	示	459
1	礼	462
3	社	180

– 4f – 王

0	王	325
1	主	123
7	理	118
	球	501
	現	326
	望	484

– 4g – 牛

0	牛	171
4	物	95
6	特	172
9	解	401

– 4h – 方

0	方	94
4	放	415
6	旅	151
7	族	150

– 4i – 夂

2	冬	221
	処	577
5	政	404
6	教	160
7	夏	223
	務	300
8	散	516
9	数	295
10	愛	309

– 4j – 欠

0	欠	365
7	欲	576
10	歌	202

– 4k – 心

0	心	102
3	忙	598
5	性	257
	怖	617
	怒	611
6	息	587
	恐	612
7	悪	178
8	情	291
	悲	564
9	想	267
	感	312
11	慣	544

– 4m – 戸

3	戻	586
4	所	270

– 4n – 戈

2	成	311
3	式	422
8	越	555
	幾	534
9	戦	328
	歳	403

– 5a – 石

0	石	252
4	研	247
5	破	480
10	確	451

– 5b – 立

0	立	111

Index by Readings

– A –

Reading	Kanji	No.
abu(nai)	危	426
a(garu)	上	29
a(geru)	上	29
AI	愛	309
ai-	相	266
-aida	間	35
aji	味	179
aji(wau)	味	179
aka	赤	144
aka(i)	赤	144
aka(rameru)	赤	144
aka(ramu)	赤	144
	明	81
a(kari)	明	81
aka(rui)	明	81
aka(rumu)	明	81
a(kasu)	明	81
a(keru)	空	117
	明	81
	開	203
aki	秋	224
akina(u)	商	378
aki(raka)	明	81
AKU	悪	178
a(ku)	空	117
	明	81
	開	203
a(kuru)	明	81
ama	天	73
	雨	27
ama(ru)	余	568
ama(su)	余	568
ame	天	73
	雨	27
AN	暗	350
(音)		ON
	安	105
	行	49
ane	姉	206
ani	兄	205
ao	青	145
ao(i)	青	145
araso(u)	争	329
ara(ta)	新	135
ara(u)	洗	491
arawa(reru)	表	317
	現	326
arawa(su)	表	317
	現	326
a(ru)	在	315
	有	166
aru(ku)	歩	211
asa	朝	225
ashi	足	90
aso(bu)	遊	556

Reading	Kanji	No.
ata(eru)	与	429
atai	値	386
atama	頭	319
atara(shii)	新	135
a(taru)	当	251
a(teru)	当	251
ato	後	39
atsu(i)	熱	470
atsu(maru)	集	213
atsu(meru)	集	213
a(u)	合	272
	会	125
a(waseru)	合	272
a(wasu)	合	272
aya(bumu)	危	426
ayama(chi)	過	379
ayama(ru)	誤	541
ayama(tsu)	過	379
aya(ui)	危	426
ayu(mu)	歩	211
aza	字	107

– B –

Reading	Kanji	No.
BA	馬場	322
ba	場	122
BAI	買	159
	売	158
ba(kasu)	化	307
ba(keru)	化	307
BAN	判	562
(半)		HAN
	番	280
	晩	503
	万	16
BATSU	抜	615
(友)		YŪ
(髪)		HATSU
	末	330
BEI	米	294
BEN	便	343
(更)		KŌ
	勉	242
BETSU	別	167
BI	美	375
	備	517
BIN	便	343
(更)		KŌ
	貧	511
(分)		BUN
BO	暮	602
	母	66
BŌ	亡	483
	忘	599
	忙	598
	望	484

Reading	Kanji	No.
BOKU	木	20
	目	88
BU	舞	523
	部	254
	不	100
	分	32
	歩	211
BUN	分	32
	文	108
	聞	47
BUTSU	物	95
BYAKU	白	75
BYŌ	猫	605
	病	201
	平	289

– C –

Reading	Kanji	No.
CHA	茶	162
CHAKU	着	239
(差)		SA
CHI	値	386
	置	387
(直)		CHOKU
	治	407
(台)		DAI
(始)		SHI
	知	147
	地	110
	恥	614
	遅	493
	質	137
chi	千	15
chichi	父	67
chiga(eru)	違	525
chiga(u)	違	525
chii(sai)	小	25
chika(i)	近	216
chikara	力	104
chi(rakaru)	散	516
chi(rakasu)	散	516
chi(rasu)	散	516
chi(ru)	散	516
CHO	緒	533
(者)		SHA
(都)		TO
CHŌ	町	139
	頂	603
	長	60
	朝	225
	調	346
	鳥	174
	重	153
CHOKU	直	385
(値)		CHI
CHŪ	注	196

Reading	Kanji	No.
(主)		SHU
	中	26
	昼	226
-CHŪ	中	26

– D –

Reading	Kanji	No.
DA	打	559
DAI	代	165
(貸)		TAI
	大	24
(太)		TAI
	弟	204
	台	229
	内	253
	題	195
DAN	男	61
(田)		DEN
	談	450
	段	355
	断	561
da(su)	出	44
DE	弟	204
DEN	田	84
	電	64
	伝	390
de(ru)	出	44
DO	努	610
	怒	611
	度	200
(席)		SEKI
(渡)		TO
	土	22
DŌ	動	156
	働	298
(重)		CHŌ
	道	120
(首)		SHU
	同	141
	堂	231
DOKU	読	77
(売)		BAI
(続)		ZOKU

– E –

Reading	Kanji	No.
E	会	125
	絵	348
	回	256
-e	重	153
EI	英	194
	映	193
	泳	583
(水)		SUI
EKI	役	361
	易	513
	駅	173
e(mu)	笑	585
EN	遠	395
	園	396
	円	13
	煙	545
	演	347
era(bu)	選	522
era(i)	偉	566
e(ru)	得	360
ETSU	越	555

– F –

Reading	Kanji	No.
FU	富	499
(福)		FUKU
	婦	336
(帰)		KI
	父	67
(交)		KŌ
	付	283
	夫	335
	怖	617
	浮	547
	不	100
	歩	211
	負	413
	風	83
FŪ	風	83
	富	499
(福)		FU
	夫	335
fu(eru)	増	498
fuka(i)	深	428
fuka(maru)	深	428
fuka(meru)	深	428
fu(kasu)	更	557
fu(keru)	老	430
	更	557
FUKU	福	600
(富)		FU
	服	240
(報)		HŌ
	腹	593
fu(ku)	吹	590
fumi	文	108
FUN	分	32
funa	船	362
fune	船	362
fu(ru)	降	549
furu(i)	古	134
furu(su)	古	134
futa-	二	3
futa(tsu)	二	3
futo(i)	太	466
futo(ru)	太	466

Reading	Kanji	No.
FUTSU	払	448
fu(yasu)	増	498
fuyu	冬	221

– G –

Reading	Kanji	No.
GA	画	191
GA'	合	272
GAI	外	58
	(夕)	SEKI
	害	418
	(割)	KATSU
GAKU	学	65
	(字)	JI
	楽	197
	(薬)	YAKU
GAN	元	115
	(完)	KAN
	願	447
	(原)	GEN
	顔	320
	(産)	SAN
GATSU	月	17
gawa	側	455
GE	下	28
	外	58
	夏	223
	解	401
GEI	迎	567
GEN	限	530
	(銀)	GIN
	(眼)	MIN
	原	264
	(願)	GAN
	験	233
	(険)	KEN
	元	115
	(完)	KAN
	言	93
	(信)	SHIN
	現	326
	(見)	KEN
GETSU	月	17
GI	議	323
	疑	608
GIN	銀	181
	(金)	KIN
GO	午	40
	御	495
	(許)	KYO
	(牛)	GYU
	五	7
	語	48
	期	398
	互	542
	後	39

Reading	Kanji	No.
GŌ	合	272
	(給)	KYŪ
	(答)	TŌ
	(今)	KON
	(会)	KAI
	号	314
	強	148
	業	169
GON	言	93
	勤	440
	権	345
GU	具	384
	(真)	SHIN
GŪ	偶	613
GYO	御	495
	(午)	GO
	(許)	KYO
	魚	176
GYŌ	行	49
	形	371
	業	169
GYŪ	牛	171
	(午)	GO

– H –

Reading	Kanji	No.
HA	破	480
	(彼)	HI
	(疲)	HI
HA'	法	262
ha	葉	306
	歯	402
HACHI	八	10
ha(eru)	生	36
	映	193
haguku(mu)	育	303
haha	母	66
HAI	背	592
	(北)	HOKU
	敗	414
	杯	580
	配	416
hai(ru)	入	43
haji	恥	614
haji(maru)	始	230
haji(me)	初	485
haji(meru)	始	230
haji(mete)	初	485
ha(jirau)	恥	614
ha(jiru)	恥	614
haka(rau)	計	190
haka(ru)	図	189
	計	190
hako	箱	573
hako(bu)	運	214
HAKU	白	75

Reading	Kanji	No.
HAN	反	340
	阪	394
	飯	185
	(返)	HEN
	半	59
	判	562
	犯	535
hana	花	164
hana(reru)	放	415
hanashi	話	76
hana(su)	放	415
	話	76
hana(tsu)	放	415
hara	原	264
	腹	593
ha(rasu)	晴	478
hara(u)	払	448
ha(reru)	晴	478
haru	春	222
hashi(ru)	走	210
hata	機	423
hatara(ku)	働	298
ha(tasu)	果	405
ha(te)	果	405
ha(teru)	果	405
HATSU	髪	579
	(友)	YŪ
	発	101
hatsu-	初	485
haya(i)	早	161
	速	411
haya(maru)	早	161
	速	411
haya(meru)	早	161
	速	411
ha(yasu)	生	36
ha(zukashii)	恥	614
hazu(reru)	外	58
hazu(su)	外	58
HEI	閉	372
	(才)	SAI
	病	201
	平	289
	返	393
HEN	変	308
	経	433
HI	彼	553
	疲	596
	(破)	HA
	非	409
	悲	564
	否	588
	(不)	FU
	飛	424
	費	509
hi	火	18

Reading	Kanji	No.
	日	5
hidari	左	55
hi(eru)	冷	526
higashi	東	51
hikari	光	265
hika(ru)	光	265
hi(keru)	引	293
hi(ku)	引	293
HIN	品	155
	(口)	KŌ
	貧	511
	(分)	BUN
hira	平	289
hira(keru)	開	203
hira(ku)	開	203
hiro(garu)	広	241
hiro(geru)	広	241
hiro(i)	広	241
hiro(maru)	広	241
hiro(meru)	広	241
hiru	昼	226
hito	人	1
hito-	一	2
hito(shii)	等	442
hito(tsu)	一	2
HITSU	必	420
hi(ya)	冷	526
hi(yakasu)	冷	526
hi(yasu)	冷	526
HO	歩	211
	(止)	SHI
	(少)	SHŌ
	捕	537
ho	火	18
HO'	法	262
HŌ	方	94
	放	415
	訪	582
	報	488
	(幸)	KŌ
	(服)	FUKU
	法	262
	(去)	KYO
	包	594
hodo	程	381
hoka	外	58
	他	260
HOKU	北	53
HON	反	340
	本	23
hō(ru)	放	415
ho(shii)	欲	576
hos(suru)	欲	576
HOTSU	発	101
HYAKU	百	14
	(白)	HAKU
HYŌ	表	317

– I –

Reading	Kanji	No.
I	偉	566
	違	525
	位	261
	(立)	RITSU
	意	114
	(音)	IN
	医	149
	易	513
I-	以	86
ICHI	一	2
ichi	市	279
ie	家	130
ika(ru)	怒	611
i(kasu)	生	36
i(keru)	生	36
iki	息	587
i(kiru)	生	36
IKU	育	303
iku	幾	534
i(ku)	行	49
ikusa	戦	328
ima	今	42
imōto	妹	207
IN	員	128
	音	192
	院	238
	(完)	KAN
	因	437
	引	293
	飲	184
ina	否	588
inochi	命	445
inu	犬	170
i(reru)	入	43
iro	色	142
i(ru)	入	43
	居	275
	要	383
ishi	石	252
isoga(shii)	忙	598
iso(gu)	急	177
itadaki	頂	603
itada(ku)	頂	603
ita(i)	痛	595
ita(meru)	痛	595
ita(mu)	痛	595
ITSU	一	2
itsu-	五	7
itsu(tsu)	五	7
i(u)	言	93

– J –

Reading	Kanji	No.
JAKU	若	431

Reading	Kanji	No./Ref.
	(右)	YŪ
	着	239
	(差)	SA
JI	持	217
	時	34
	(待)	TAI
	(等)	TŌ
	治	407
	(台)	DAI
	(始)	SHI
	次	366
	(欠)	KETSU
	(吹)	SUI
	除	569
	(余)	YO
	示	459
	(元)	GEN
	字	107
	(子)	SHI
	自	92
	(目)	MOKU
	似	606
	(以)	I
	地	110
	仕	188
	耳	248
	辞	489
	事	96
JI'	十	12
-ji	路	269
JIKI	直	385
	食	79
JIN	人	1
	(入)	NYŪ
	神	333
	(申)	SHIN
JITSU	日	5
	実	290
JO	除	569
	(余)	JO
	女	62
	助	464
JŌ	静	479
	情	291
	(青)	SEI
	(精)	SEI
	(争)	SŌ
	常	408
	(堂)	DŌ
	状	465
	(犬)	KEN
	成	311
	乗	421
	定	351
	場	122
	上	29
JU	受	310
JŪ	住	124
	(主)	SHU
	(注)	CHŪ
	十	12
	(計)	KEI
	重	153
	中	26
-JŪ		
JUTSU	術	281

– K –

Reading	Kanji	No./Ref.
KA	可	369
	何	80
	歌	202
	化	307
	花	164
	靴	571
	科	338
	(料)	RYŌ
	果	405
	家	130
	過	379
	加	496
	下	28
	火	18
	夏	223
	合	272
KA'	日	5
-ka	代	165
ka(eru)	変	308
	返	393
kae(ru)	帰	182
	返	393
kae(su)	帰	182
kagi(ru)	限	530
KAI	会	125
	絵	348
	海	109
	(毎)	MAI
	界	219
	皆	449
	解	401
	回	256
	開	203
kakari	係	543
	掛	604
ka(karu)	掛	604
kaka(ru)	係	543
kaka(waru)	関	373
ka(keru)	欠	365
	掛	604
KAKU	客	468
	格	469
	覚	453
	(見)	KEN
	画	191
	確	451
ka(ku)	欠	365
	書	70
kama(eru)	構	558
kama(u)	構	558
kami	上	29
	神	333
	紙	138
	髪	579
	官	341
KAN	館	186
	間	35
	関	373
	観	452
	(権)	KEN
	完	458
	(元)	GAN
	漢	236
	(難)	NAN
	感	312
	慣	544
	寒	400
kan	神	333
kana	金	21
kaname	要	383
kanara(zu)	必	420
kana(shii)	悲	564
kana(shimu)	悲	564
kane	金	21
kanga(eru)	考	235
kano	彼	553
kao	顔	320
kara	空	117
karada	体	91
kare	彼	553
ka(riru)	借	244
kasa(naru)	重	153
kasa(neru)	重	153
kashira	頭	319
ka(su)	貸	243
kata	形	371
	方	94
katachi	形	371
kata(i)	難	438
kata(rau)	語	48
kata(ru)	語	48
KATSU	活	301
	(話)	WA
	割	419
	(害)	GAI
ka(tsu)	勝	412
ka(u)	交	259
	買	159
kawa	川	30
ka(waru)	代	165
	変	308
ka(wasu)	交	259
kayo(u)	通	121
kaza	風	83
kaze	風	83
kazo(eru)	数	295
kazu	数	295
KE	化	307
	気	72
	家	130
	京	140
KEI	景	532
	経	433
	形	371
	係	543
	警	494
	兄	205
	計	190
kemu(i)	煙	545
kemuri	煙	545
kemu(ru)	煙	545
KEN	険	425
	験	233
	権	345
	(観)	KAN
	件	502
	(牛)	GYŪ
	建	245
	犬	170
	見	46
	研	247
	間	35
ke(su)	消	528
KETSU	決	352
	欠	365
kewa(shii)	険	425
KI	起	199
	記	359
	幾	534
	機	423
	帰	182
	(婦)	FU
	気	72
	期	398
	寄	597
	危	426
	規	454
	喜	578
ki	木	20
ki-	生	36
ki(eru)	消	528
ki(koeru)	聞	47
ki(ku)	聞	47
	利	342
ki(maru)	決	352
ki(meru)	決	352
kimi	君	521
KIN	勤	440
	金	21
	今	42
	近	216
ki(reru)	切	85
ki(ru)	切	85
	着	239
ki(seru)	着	239
kita	北	53
kita(ru)	来	50
kita(su)	来	50
kiwa	際	460
kiwa(meru)	究	246
kiza(mu)	刻	584
KO	古	134
	(居)	KYO
	去	208
	呼	589
ko	子	63
	木	20
ko-	小	25
KŌ	口	87
	向	286
	高	74
	格	469
	交	259
	校	68
	(父)	FU
	公	113
	広	241
	行	49
	後	39
	港	481
	(共)	KYŌ
	(供)	KYŌ
	更	557
	(便)	BEN
	工	116
	好	258
	考	235
	候	548
	構	558
	降	549
	光	265
	幸	487
kō	神	333
koe	声	508
ko(eru)	越	555
kokono-	九	11
kokono(tsu)	九	11
kokoro	心	102
kokoro(miru)	試	232
KOKU	告	490
	刻	584
	国	33
	黒	143
	石	252
koma(ru)	困	439
kome	米	294

Reading	Kanji	No.
ko(meru)	込	518
ko(mu)	込	518
KON	困	439
	(木)	BOKU
	(因)	IN
	建	245
	今	42
	金	21
	婚	441
kono(mu)	好	258
koro(bu)	転	212
koro(garu)	転	212
koro(gasu)	転	212
koro(geru)	転	212
koro(su)	殺	444
ko(su)	越	555
kota(e)	答	126
kota(eru)	答	126
koto	事	96
-koto	言	93
kotowa(ru)	断	561
kowa-	声	508
kowa(i)	怖	617
KU	工	116
	(空)	KŪ
	供	285
	(共)	KYŌ
	苦	432
	(古)	KO
	九	11
	口	87
KŪ	空	117
kuba(ru)	配	416
kubi	首	268
kuchi	口	87
kuda(ru)	下	28
kuda(saru)	下	28
kuda(su)	下	28
kumi	組	382
ku(mu)	組	382
KUN	君	521
kuni	国	33
kurai	位	261
kura(i)	暗	350
ku(rasu)	暮	602
ku(rau)	食	79
ku(reru)	暮	602
kuro	黒	143
kuro(i)	黒	143
ku(ru)	来	50
kuruma	車	71
kuru(shii)	苦	432
kuru(shimeru)	苦	432
kuru(shimu)	苦	432
kusa	草	305
kusuri	薬	353
kutsu	靴	571
ku(u)	食	79
kuwa(eru)	加	496
kuwa(waru)	加	496
KYAKU	客	468
KYO	去	208
	(土)	DO
	居	275
	(古)	KO
	許	504
	(午)	GO
KYŌ	共	284
	供	285
	兄	205
	京	140
	経	433
	教	160
	恐	612
	強	148
KYOKU	曲	358
	局	274
KYŪ	求	500
	球	501
	九	11
	究	246
	休	45
	(木)	BOKU
	給	349
	(合)	GŌ
	急	177
	吸	591

– M –

Reading	Kanji	No.
ma	目	88
	真	209
	馬	322
	間	35
machi	町	139
mado	窓	492
mae	前	38
ma(garu)	曲	358
ma(geru)	曲	358
MAI	妹	207
	(未)	MI
	(味)	MI
	(末)	MATSU
	毎	69
	(母)	BO
	(海)	KAI
	米	294
mai	舞	523
mai(ru)	参	497
maji(eru)	交	259
ma(jiru)	交	259
maji(waru)	交	259
maka(seru)	任	344
	負	413
maka(su)	任	344
ma(keru)	負	413
mamo(ru)	守	406
MAN	万	16
	満	288
mana(bu)	学	65
mane(ku)	招	399
maru(i)	円	13
masa (ni)	正	168
masa(ru)	勝	412
ma(su)	増	498
mato	的	146
MATSU	末	330
	(未)	MI
ma(tsu)	待	218
matsurigoto	政	404
matta(ku)	全	255
ma(u)	舞	523
mawa(ru)	回	256
mawa(su)	回	256
mayo(u)	迷	552
ma(zaru)	交	259
ma(zeru)	交	259
mazu(shii)	貧	511
me	女	62
	目	88
MEI	命	445
	(念)	NEN
	迷	552
	(米)	BEI
	鳴	546
	(鳥)	CHŌ
	名	57
	明	81
MEN	面	318
meshi	飯	185
MI	未	331
	味	179
	(妹)	MAI
	(末)	MATSU
mi	身	249
	実	290
mi-	三	4
michi	道	120
mi(chiru)	満	288
mi(eru)	見	46
migi	右	56
mimi	耳	248
MIN	民	276
	眠	531
mina	皆	449
minami	南	54
minato	港	481
mino(ru)	実	290
mi(ru)	見	46
mise	店	133
mi(seru)	見	46
mi(tasu)	満	288
mito(meru)	認	505
mi(tsu)	三	4
mit(tsu)	三	4
miyako	都	282
mizu	水	19
mizuka(ra)	自	92
MŌ	亡	483
	望	484
mochi(iru)	用	106
modo(ru)	戻	586
modo(su)	戻	586
MOKU	木	20
	目	88
MON	問	127
	聞	47
	(間)	KAN
	文	108
mono	者	129
	物	95
mori	守	406
mo(shikuwa)	若	431
mō(su)	申	332
moto	下	28
	元	115
	本	23
moto(meru)	求	500
MOTSU	物	95
mo(tsu)	持	217
motto(mo)	最	313
MU	務	300
	(予)	YO
	夢	524
	(夕)	YŪ
mu-	六	8
mui-	六	8
muka(eru)	迎	567
mukashi	昔	515
mu(kau)	向	286
mu(keru)	向	286
mu(kō)	向	286
mu(ku)	向	286
muku(iru)	報	488
muro	室	131
musume	娘	616
mu(tsu)	六	8
mut(tsu)	六	8
muzuka(shii)	難	438
MYŌ	命	445
	(念)	NEN
	名	57
	明	81

– N –

Reading	Kanji	No.
NA	南	54
na	名	57
naga(i)	長	60
naga(reru)	流	304
naga(su)	流	304
na(geru)	投	560
nago(mu)	和	263
nago(yaka)	和	263
NAI	内	253
na(i)	亡	483
naka	中	26
naka(ba)	半	59
na(ku)	鳴	546
nama	生	36
NAN	難	438
	(漢)	KAN
	南	54
	男	61
nan	何	80
nana-	七	9
nana(tsu)	七	9
nani	何	80
nano-	七	9
nao(ru)	直	385
	治	407
nao(su)	直	385
	治	407
na(rasu)	鳴	546
	慣	544
nara(u)	習	237
na(reru)	慣	544
na(ru)	成	311
	鳴	546
nasa(ke)	情	291
na(su)	成	311
natsu	夏	223
ne	音	192
	値	386
nega(u)	願	447
ne(kasu)	寝	572
neko	猫	605
nemu(i)	眠	531
nemu(ru)	眠	531
NEN	念	446
	(今)	KON
	(命)	MEI
	然	472
	年	37
ne(ru)	寝	572
NETSU	熱	470
NI	二	3
NICHI	日	5
niga(i)	苦	432
niga(ru)	苦	432
ni(gasu)	逃	609
ni(geru)	逃	609
nii-	新	135
NIKU	肉	152

Reading	Kanji	Page
	(内)	NAI
NIN	任	344
	認	505
	人	1
ni(ru)	似	606
nishi	西	52
niwa	庭	575
no	野	157
NŌ	能	368
nobo(ru)	上	29
	登	551
nobo(seru)	上	29
nobo(su)	上	29
nochi	後	39
noga(reru)	逃	609
noga(su)	逃	609
noko(ru)	残	471
noko(su)	残	471
no(mu)	飲	184
no(ru)	乗	421
no(seru)	乗	421
nozo(ku)	除	569
nozo(mu)	望	484
nu(karu)	抜	615
nu(kasu)	抜	615
nu(keru)	抜	615
nu(ku)	抜	615
nushi	主	123
nusu(mu)	盗	574
NYAKU	若	431
NYO	女	62
NYŌ	女	62
NYŪ	入	43
	(人)	JIN

– O –

Reading	Kanji	Page
O	悪	178
	和	263
o	緒	533
o-	小	25
Ō	王	325
	横	519
	押	554
ō-	大	24
obo(eru)	覚	453
o(chiru)	落	527
o(eru)	終	220
ō(i)	多	154
ō(i ni)	大	24
o(iru)	老	430
oka(su)	犯	535
ō(kii)	大	24
o(kiru)	起	199
okona(u)	行	49
oko(ru)	怒	611
o(koru)	起	199
o(kosu)	起	199
OKU	屋	132
o(ku)	置	387
oku(rasu)	遅	493
oku(reru)	後	39
	遅	493
oku(ru)	送	215
omo	主	123
	面	318
omo(i)	重	153
omote	表	317
	面	318
omo(u)	思	103
ON	遠	395
	(園)	EN
	音	192
on-	御	495
ona(ji)	同	141
onna	女	62
o(reru)	折	601
ori	折	601
o(riru)	下	28
	降	549
o(rosu)	下	28
o(ru)	折	601
osa(maru)	収	512
	治	407
osa(meru)	収	512
	治	407
oshi(eru)	教	160
oso(i)	遅	493
oso(reru)	恐	612
oso(roshii)	恐	612
oso(waru)	教	160
o(su)	押	554
oto	音	192
otoko	男	61
o(tosu)	落	527
otōto	弟	204
otozu(reru)	訪	582
otto	夫	335
o(u)	生	36
	追	581
	負	413
o(waru)	終	220
oya	親	136
ōyake	公	113
oyo(gu)	泳	583

– R –

Reading	Kanji	Page
RAI	礼	462
	来	50
	頼	607
RAKU	楽	197
	(薬)	YAKU
	落	527
REI	例	457
	(列)	RETSU
	冷	526
	礼	462
	戻	586
REN	連	392
	(車)	SHA
RETSU	列	456
	(例)	REI
RI	理	118
	利	342
RIKI	力	104
RITSU	立	111
RO	路	269
	(足)	SOKU
RŌ	老	430
	(考)	KŌ
	労	299
	(力)	RYOKU
ROKU	六	8
RON	論	324
RU	留	514
	流	304
RUI	類	296
RYO	旅	151
	(族)	ZOKU
RYŌ	料	183
	(科)	KA
	両	287
	良	339
RYOKU	力	104
RYŪ	立	111
	留	514
	流	304

– S –

Reading	Kanji	Page
SA	左	55
	差	476
	(着)	CHAKU
	作	198
	(昨)	SAKU
	茶	162
SA'	早	161
sachi	幸	487
sada(ka)	定	351
sada(maru)	定	351
sada(meru)	定	351
sa(garu)	下	28
saga(su)	探	427
sa(geru)	下	28
sagu(ru)	探	427
SAI	才	435
	財	436
	際	460
	(察)	SATSU
	最	313
	(取)	SHU
	西	52
	切	85
	歳	403
	済	434
	妻	482
	殺	444
saiwa(i)	幸	487
saka	酒	417
sakana	魚	176
sakazuki	杯	580
sake	酒	417
saki	先	41
SAKU	作	198
	昨	354
sa(ku)	割	419
sama	様	376
-sama	様	376
sa(masu)	冷	526
	覚	453
sa(meru)	冷	526
	覚	453
samu(i)	寒	400
SAN	産	321
	(生)	SEI
	散	516
	(昔)	SEKI
	参	497
	賛	507
	三	4
	山	31
sara	更	557
sa(ru)	去	208
sasa(eru)	支	337
sa(su)	指	565
	差	476
SATSU	察	461
	(際)	SAI
	殺	444
SE	世	163
se	背	592
SEI	青	145
	情	291
	晴	478
	静	479
	精	477
	生	36
	性	257
	(産)	SAN
	正	168
	政	404
	成	311
	制	388
	世	163
	西	52
	声	508
	歳	403
sei	背	592
SEKI	責	474
	積	475
	昔	515
	(借)	SHAKU
	席	364
	(度)	DO
	赤	144
	夕	97
	石	252
seki	関	373
se(meru)	責	474
SEN	先	41
	洗	491
	選	522
	川	30
	千	15
	船	362
	戦	328
SETSU	殺	444
	説	374
	切	85
	折	601
	雪	550
SHA	者	129
	写	234
	(与)	YO
	社	180
	車	71
SHAKU	昔	515
	借	244
	石	252
	赤	144
SHI	市	279
	姉	206
	師	377
	次	366
	資	510
	(欠)	KETSU
	止	228
	歯	402
	私	112
	(払)	FUTSU
	始	230
	(台)	TAI
	(治)	JI
	試	232
	(式)	SHIKI
	子	63
	四	6
	死	98
	仕	188

Reading	Kanji	No.
	支	337
	指	565
	使	187
	紙	138
	示	459
	自	92
	思	103
shiawa(se)	幸	487
SHICHI	七	9
	質	137
shi(iru)	強	148
SHIKI	識	486
	色	142
	式	422
shi(maru)	閉	372
shi(meru)	閉	372
shime(su)	示	459
shimo	下	28
SHIN	新	135
	親	136
	申	332
	神	333
	心	102
	(必)	HITSU
	深	428
	(探)	TAN
	身	249
	信	271
	進	391
	寝	572
	真	209
shina	品	155
shi(nu)	死	98
shira	白	75
shira(beru)	調	346
shirizo(keru)	退	529
shirizo(ku)	退	529
shiro	代	165
	白	75
shiro(i)	白	75
shi(ru)	知	147
shiru(su)	記	359
shita	下	28
shita(shii)	親	136
shita(shimu)	親	136
SHITSU	失	334
	(医)	I
	室	131
	(屋)	OKU
	質	137
shizu	静	479
shizu(ka)	静	479
shizu(maru)	静	479
shizu(meru)	静	479
SHO	緒	533
	(者)	SHA
	処	577
	初	485

Reading	Kanji	No.
	所	270
	書	70
SHŌ	青	145
	精	477
	(情)	JŌ
	(晴)	SEI
	(静)	JŌ
	小	25
	少	119
	(歩)	HO
	生	36
	性	257
	正	168
	政	404
	相	266
	(想)	SŌ
	消	528
	招	399
	勝	412
	上	29
	声	508
	笑	585
	商	378
SHOKU	職	367
	(識)	SHIKI
	食	79
	色	142
	主	123
	(王)	Ō
SHU	首	268
	(目)	MOKU
	種	297
	(重)	JŪ
	酒	417
	守	406
	取	250
	手	89
	週	99
	(調)	CHŌ
SHŪ	終	220
	(冬)	TŌ
	収	512
	秋	224
	集	213
	習	237
SHUKU	宿	278
SHUN	春	222
SHUTSU	出	44
SO	祖	463
	組	382
	想	267
	(相)	SŌ
SŌ	相	266
	想	267
	早	161
	草	305
	走	210
	送	215

Reading	Kanji	No.
	窓	492
	(公)	KŌ
	争	329
soda(teru)	育	303
soda(tsu)	育	303
SOKU	束	410
	速	411
	息	587
	側	455
	足	90
-so(meru)	初	485
somu(keru)	背	592
somu(ku)	背	592
SON	存	316
	(在)	ZAI
sona(eru)	供	285
	備	517
sona(waru)	備	517
sono	園	396
sora	空	117
so(rasu)	反	340
sōrō	候	548
so(ru)	反	340
soso(gu)	注	196
soto	外	58
SU	主	123
	(王)	Ō
	子	63
	守	406
	数	295
SŪ	数	295
sube(te)	全	255
sue	末	330
su(giru)	過	379
su(gosu)	過	379
sugu(reru)	優	563
SUI	吹	590
	(欠)	KETSU
	水	19
	出	44
suke	助	464
suko(shi)	少	119
su(ku)	好	258
	少	119
suku(nai)	少	119
su(masu)	済	434
su(mau)	住	124
sumi(yaka)	速	411
su(mu)	済	434
	住	124
susu(meru)	進	391
susu(mu)	進	391
su(u)	吸	591
suwa(ru)	座	520

– T –

Reading	Kanji	No.
TA	太	466
	(大)	TAI
	他	260
	多	154
ta	手	89
	田	84
taba	束	410
ta(beru)	食	79
tabi	度	200
	旅	151
tada(chi ni)	直	385
tada(shii)	正	168
tada(su)	正	168
ta(eru)	絶	506
taga(i)	互	542
tagu(i)	類	296
TAI	対	357
	待	218
	(持)	JI
	(時)	JI
	大	24
	太	466
	代	165
	貸	243
	台	229
	(治)	JI
	(始)	SHI
	体	91
	(本)	HON
	(休)	KYŪ
	退	529
tai(ra)	平	289
taka	高	74
taka(i)	高	74
taka(maru)	高	74
taka(meru)	高	74
TAKU	度	200
	(席)	SEKI
	宅	277
tama	球	501
tame(su)	試	232
tami	民	276
TAN	単	327
	(戦)	SEN
	探	427
	(深)	SHIN
	反	340
tane	種	297
tano(moshii)	頼	607
tano(mu)	頼	607
tano(shii)	楽	197
tano(shimu)	楽	197
tao(reru)	倒	540
tao(su)	倒	540
ta(riru)	足	90
ta(ru)	足	90
tashi(ka)	確	451

Reading	Kanji	No.
tashi(kameru)	確	451
ta(su)	足	90
tasu(karu)	助	464
tasu(keru)	助	464
tataka(u)	戦	328
ta(teru)	立	111
	建	245
tato(eru)	例	457
TATSU	達	397
ta(tsu)	立	111
	建	245
	断	561
	絶	506
ta(yasu)	絶	506
tayo(ri)	便	343
tayo(ru)	頼	607
tazu(neru)	訪	582
te	手	89
TEI	体	91
	(本)	HON
	(休)	KYŪ
	弟	204
	庭	575
	定	351
	程	381
TEKI	的	146
	(約)	YAKU
	適	380
TEN	店	133
	点	273
	転	212
	(伝)	DEN
TO	天	73
	度	200
	渡	363
	(席)	SEKI
	登	551
	頭	319
	途	570
	(余)	YO
	都	282
	(者)	SHA
	徒	389
	(走)	SŌ
to-	土	22
	図	189
	十	12
TŌ	登	551
	頭	319
	到	539
	倒	540
	読	77
	(売)	BAI
	(続)	ZOKU
	答	126
	(合)	GŌ

The 79 Radicals

2	亻a	氵b	孑c	阝d	卩e	刂f	力g	又h	宀i	亠j
	十k	卜m	夂n	丷o	厂p	辶q	冂r	几s	匚t	

3	氵a	土b	扌c	口d	女e	巾f	犭g	弓h	彳i	彡j
	艹k	宀m	丷n	屮o	圭p	广q	尸r	囗s		

4	木a	月b	日c	火d	礻e	王f	牛g	方h	攵i	欠j
	心k	戶m	戈n							

5	石a	立b	目c	禾d	衤e	罒f	罓g	皿h	疒i	

6	糸a	米b	舟c	虫d	耳e	竹f				

7	言a	貝b	車c	足d	酉e					

8	金a	食b	隹c	雨d	門e					

9	頁a			10	馬a		11	魚a	鳥b	